MW01075562

SAINT WHO?

Saint Who?
~39 HOLY UNKNOWNS~

Brian O'Neel

SERVANT
BOOKS

PUBLISHED BY ST. ANTHONY MESSENGER PRESS
CINCINNATI, OHIO

Unless otherwise noted, Scripture passages have been taken from the *Revised Standard Version*, Catholic edition. Copyright 1946, 1952, 1971 by the Division of Christian Education of the National Council of Churches of Christ in the USA. Used by permission. All rights reserved.

Cover and book design by Mark Sullivan
Cover image:
Hemma of Gurk by Sebald Bopp, ca. 1510
© Museo Thyssen-Bornemisza, Madrid

LIBRARY OF CONGRESS CATALOGING-IN-PUBLICATION DATA
O'Neel, Brian.
Saint who? : 39 holy unknowns / Brian O'Neel.
p. cm.
Includes bibliographical references.
ISBN 978-1-61636-242-3 (pbk. : alk. paper) 1. Christian saints—Biography. 2. Blessed—Biography. 3. Christian martyrs—Biography. I. Title.
BX4655.3.O545 2012
282.092'2—dc23
[B]
2012003298
ISBN 978-1-61636-242-3

Copyright ©2012, Brian O'Neel. All rights reserved.
Published by Servant Books,
an imprint of St. Anthony Messenger Press.
28 W. Liberty St.
Cincinnati, OH 45202
www.AmericanCatholic.org
www.ServantBooks.org

Printed in the United States of America.
Printed on acid-free paper.
12 13 14 15 16   5 4 3 2 1

Contents

Dedication

First, I dedicate this book once again to my beautiful wife and children for their patient and forbearing support. A project like this takes a lot of time.

It would be the worst case of ingratitude to God ever, however, if I did not also dedicate it my former AP English teacher at Troy High School, in Fullerton, California, Mr. Fares Sawaya. He retired in 2006 after thirty-nine years in teaching, and was without question the best teacher I ever had and one of only two whom I can honestly say I loved. Without him, I mostly likely would never have become a writer. He taught so many to love that craft and any form of the written word, including Alyson Noel, author of the bestselling *The Immortals* series. She, too, credits him for her becoming a published author.

What made Mr. Sawaya so special, though, is his belief that our knowing how to write and critically read the classics of Western literature were not enough. Rather, he showed deep concern about our lives and plans. He also cared about making us well-rounded people, even, dare I say, cultured. I suspect he believed it his duty to do so.

Therefore, Mr. Saway would sometimes start class by saying, "Let's talk about some issue of the day or a philosophical question. Miss Petroff, do you think... Miss McColl, how did you find... Mr. Campanella, do you agree?"

Or Mr. Sawaya would tell us, "Put away your books. Today, we're going to listen to this." And he would take out a John Coltrane or Bach record, put it on the turntable, and turn out the lights, and we would listen, the silent darkness interwoven with these aural works, sometimes amazing, others times not. When the record finished, the light would return, he would make some points about the piece itself, and then we would discuss.

What did any of this have to do with AP English? Absolutely nothing. Then again, absolutely everything. Through such exercises, Mr. Sawaya taught us the baby steps of critical and rational thinking. And you know what? When we his former students discuss those amazing years we spent with him, each agrees to a person we are the better for it. We recognize we would have missed something tremendous were it not for him. All of us learned more from him about life, culture, and the world we would someday enter than we would have anywhere else.

One reason he retired is because state and federal laws increasingly force teachers to teach toward standardized testing. It is a school's score that is important, even if true education has to suffer. That was not Mr. Sawaya. It never could be. Now he and others like him have left, and how impoverished will be our world. Alyson and I were both aimlessly drifting and clueless until he taught us a skill few have.

Would that I could transport you back in time to those halcyon days so you could see for yourselves. A whole book could be written about this amazing, beautiful man whom I last saw in 1985 and yet idolize no less now than when I was eighteen.

Please pray for him, thank God for him, and ask that God send many others just like Mr. Fares Sawaya, because such teachers make our world such a better place.

Acknowledgments

To all at Servant Books, especially two women who are just jewels, Louise Paré and Claudia Volkman, and my editor Nicholas Frankovich, a man of foresight, prudence, and discretion. I need to also mention Chris Holmes and Lindsey Simmons, who helped my previous book, *39 New Saints You Should Know*, do as well as it did. It would be borderline sinful of me not to compliment Mark Sullivan, who I think you'll agree did a smashing job on the internal layout and the wonderful cover he designed.

Also, thanks to all who bought a copy of the last book, joined the *39 New Saints You Should Know* Facebook page, bought multiple copies for friends, came to the book signings, actually held book signings, invited me to speak, carried it in their bookstores, or otherwise did so much to support this work.

Finally, thanks to all who told me how much *39 New Saints You Should Know* meant to you. You told me this book helped you realize that your own sanctity and thus sainthood were possible, that they weren't disheartening out of reach. Few Catholic authors grow rich; I know I certainly haven't. But such comments as yours are wealth enough. From the bottom my heart, I thank you.

If you would like to share with me your thoughts on this book or *39 New Saints You Should Know*—how it impacted you, which story you liked most, etc.—please write me at catholicPBwriter@yahoo.com. This is also the address to write to schedule me for speaking engagements, media interviews, and book signings.

A final note: It is easy and sometimes even fun to make online purchases of books. However, Catholic bookstores are really hurting. Dozens if not hundreds have closed since the world's economy began turning for the worse in 2008. Therefore, if at all possible, please patronize your local Catholic bookstore. After all, potential converts will not get their questions about our Holy Faith from a customer service rep at an online big-box retailer. Catholic-bookstore owners and their employees, however, are often a potential convert's first encounter with the Church. It is highly critical, therefore, that we do our part to keep their doors open. To find one nearest you in the United States, go to http://catholicstorefinder.com/. Outside of the United States, you might try using an online search engine or calling your diocese's chancery. Good luck!

Foreword

Pope Pius VI said that today we do not listen to teachers as much as to witnesses; if we listen to teachers at all, he tells us, it is because they *are* witnesses. Since her inception, Holy Mother Church has provided us with great numbers of teachers who are witnesses. Called the saints, these men and women have risen to the altar of Christ because of their love for God displayed through heroic virtue. Like stars in the sky guiding the wayfarer along the path, their witness to the faith has taught us much about virtue and Christian living. Patience, fortitude, long-suffering, endurance, faithfulness, generosity, constancy, and hope—with all of their derivatives—have been exemplified in them to stellar proportions.

I remember well how these holy men and women influenced my life as a young girl. Fortunate to have attended Catholic school in the elementary and secondary grades, I am grateful for the religious sisters, who by their stories, enlivened my imagination and my youthful zeal. I thrilled to consider martyrdom after hearing of St. Isaac Jogues (though I did ask that my digits would remain intact!), and I was greatly inspired by the story of St. Maria Goretti. St. Thérèse of Lisieux was my favorite, and at eight years of age I wrote a poem to her. A love for the Blessed Mother, Queen of All Saints, was gestated in my heart in those young years, as was a great regard for St. Joseph, foster father of Jesus, protector and provider. And it was with wonder that I listened to a friend tell me fascinating stories of a man then living in Italy whose canonization I would live to see—Padre Pio, St. Pio of Pietrelcina. Little did I know that there were other saints alive at that same time who were about the business of saintly endeavor and whose ascent toward the altar I would witness as well—Bl. John XXIII, Bl. Teresa of Calcutta, and Bl. John Paul

II, to name the most well-known.

My fascination with the saints has not waned in my adult years, and my desire to imitate their virtues has increased within me. I find great inspiration in St. Madeleine Sophie Barat, for example, as well as St. Josephine Bakita. St. Louis de Montfort has become a spiritual mentor, and numbers of the up-and-coming saints have left an imprint on me as well—Dorothy Day, Elisabeth Leseur, and Venerable Solanus Casey among them.

While my heart obviously holds a place for all of the great saints known to us from antiquity forward, I have a growing interest in many of the lesser-known saints. For this, I owe a great deal of gratitude to Brian O'Neel. I featured him for a week's worth of episodes on my television program *Women of Grace* (seen on EWTN). *Intrigued* is the word I would use to best describe my reaction to his first book and to the witnesses of the "lesser-knowns" he shared. I was mesmerized and edified by the stories he told. Again, it proved to me the remarkable truth that in every day and time God is raising up a people to be his presence in the world. And, in our day and time, the need for his presence has never been greater. It is absolutely critical.

Pope Benedict XVI reminded the world's bishops of this reality in a letter he wrote to them in March 2009. There the Holy Father said, "In our days, when in vast areas of the world the faith is in danger of dying out like a flame that no longer has fuel, the overriding priority is to make God present in the world and to show men and women the way to God." What potent words, and yet words that Our Lord himself spoke to his apostles: "Go therefore and make disciples of all nations, baptizing them in the name of the Father and of the Son and of the Holy Spirit" (Matthew 28:19). This is the call of the Christian. This is the call of the saint. And in this, our day and time, this call belongs to you and to me.

Brian O'Neel has once again offered us an invaluable aid to make headway in our saintly endeavor. In *Saint Who? 39 Holy Unknowns*, he proves again that ordinary men and women can become extraordinary recipients of grace who bring the face of God to the world. We need not worry about our talents or lack of them. St. Romanus of Le Mans shows us that even the scatterbrained and inarticulate can be great evangelists. We need not be concerned about our state in life. St. Lydwine of Scheidam proves that every state in life is a vehicle for sanctity, even when lived from a bed of pain. We need not be concerned about misunderstanding, the malicious intentions of others, or calumny. The witness of St. Mary MacKillop proves that all things work together for the good and bring holiness and sanctity when united to the passion of Christ. These saints, and all those Mr. O'Neel introduces in this book, inspire us to move forward with faith and trust in God no matter our situation or circumstance, and to remember that with God all things are possible.

God has given us life at this moment in the history of man that we might be a saint of today, a man or woman willing to be his presence today, a North Star, who leads and guides, teaches and inspires through the witness of our lives. Let us ask all of the heavenly saints to pray for us that we might acquire the necessary virtues to be the face of God in the midst of our world as they were in theirs. And let us place ourselves under the mantle of our Blessed Lady, Queen of All Saints, who desires to pour her maternal beatitude upon us that we, like she, bring Jesus Christ to the world and the world to Jesus Christ.

Johnnette S. Benkovic
Founder and president, Women of Grace
Television and radio host, author
October 30, 2011

Introduction

Why do we need yet *another* book about saints, especially one on those who are, let's face it, saintly has-beens: forgotten, little known, ignored, and, well—dare we say it?—ultimately unimportant? After all, if they were important, wouldn't they be better known?

It's a fair question, but let me answer with another: Why do we even *have* saints?

The reason Holy Mother Church presents us with saints is that each one is a beautiful mosaic tile. Now, ordinarily, individual mosaic tiles are nothing to behold. They may be jasper, cornelian, teal, gold, or whatever, but they are just teensy little boring tiles. Saints, on the other hand, are mosaic tiles that are beautiful, breathtaking to behold on their own, even apart from the larger magnificent picture they help to create.

And what is this picture that these tens of thousands of tiles the Church has given us come together in harmony to form? It is nothing less than an icon of Christ. Through the eyes of this icon, we see Our Lord's deep love for us, his burning, plaintive longing, and desire to be yoked with us. It is the same way an ardent groom longs to be yoked to his bride on his wedding day, so that they may be one. Forever.

As I learned in the wake of the publication of my first book, *39 New Saints You Should Know*, the sad truth with most people is that they don't think they deserve to be a tile in that magnificent mosaic. But they do. They can become saints. We all can. And the saints—each and every saint—show us how.

Every time the Church presents us with yet another mosaic tile, it is like a parent urging on a child who is learning to walk. "Come on. You can do it. That's it. Good boy! Good girl! I'm so *proud* of you!" She's encouraging us on this earthly pilgrimage, step by step, to stay toddling on a path where our lives will become more and more conformed to Christ. That's why she gives us saints.

The problem, however, is that those who have gone before us—who have already been presented as examples for our edification, who have already been fitted into their proper places in that icon of Christ—tend to get lost in the shuffle, don't they? It is as if we would look at this or that area of the icon and declare, "This part of the picture isn't important." But that's not true, is it?

This book is an attempt to help us step back and see some of Christianity's greatest hits from ages past. It will let us recall their places in our spiritual genealogy and family history.

But that's not all. If all we know is the story, that does us no more good than an old, cracked, sepia-toned picture, set in a frame on a wall in the hallway, of some ancestor with whom we have only a vague familiarity. What is most important is that we understand the lessons they present and use those to become saints, to become magnificent tiles that point others to the icon of Christ. In other words, we need to find the instructive thread in each of their stories. It is my hope this book helps all of us do that, because, forgotten or no, the lessons these men and women teach us are timeless.

But just how did these people become so obscure? After all, some were their age's holy equivalent of a major celebrity. Everyone knew of them. Their tombs drew immense crowds of pilgrims.

Let me give you an example. During our 2003 pilgrimage to Rome, my wife wanted to get out of the Eternal City and see something different, something that wasn't touristy, some place imbued with Old World charm and history. After doing some research, she settled on Orvieto.

"Orvieto? Where is *that*?" I sniffed.

"It's about an hour from Rome," she said. "Don't worry. You'll love it."

And she was right. Orvieto is a magical town, truly an enchanting place that time seems to have forgotten. It affords freedom to roam and wonderful surprises down every street. Plus, its stunning cathedral houses a eucharistic miracle.

Not long afterward, though, I learned it houses something else. On returning home, I did research to learn more about the city. That is how I happened on the man who started the idea for this book.

"San Pietro Parenzo," or St. Peter Parenzo, was once a big reason people came to this town on the Umbrian plain. During the Middle Ages, *millions* of pilgrims came to his tomb to seek miracles, and plenty received them. Today, however, how many have even heard of this man? Furthermore, he is not Orvieto's only forgotten saint.

During this pilgrimage I would gleefully hop from church to church, eager to investigate whatever each had to offer. It was midday during our trip to Orvieto, and we had just bought some deli cuts and bread from a butcher and sat down on the step to eat *pranzo*. Suddenly, just as I was about to take my first bite, I spied another church out of the corner of my eye.

My forbearing wife, meanwhile, had become "churched out" by the fourth day of our trip. She rolled her eyes and waved me off. I dashed over to this latest find and darted inside.

The little *chiesa* was nothing special. It was quaint but somewhat stark compared to the sumptuous beauty we had seen elsewhere. But as I walked down the nave, I spied an altar on the right, and I could tell a body was encased in glass beneath it. That meant a saint! Pay dirt! I made my way over with heart-pounding anticipation, hoping to see some great hero of the faith.

And well he may have been at some point, but I had never heard of Bl. Tommaso da Orvieto. Not many others have either, evidently, because until recently I found little evidence that he even existed.

Thus it is with many of those officially recognized as being before the beatific vision. Some saints, like Pietro, were universally well-known for a time. Others, like Tommaso, were the objects of local or regional veneration. Still others were never that well-known but nonetheless had an immense impact on their age.

Some were forgotten because of the vagaries of human whim. The cult of others was dependent on there being a shrine to their memory, and once the shrine was bypassed by a different road or destroyed by Reformers or revolutionaries, so was their remembrance. Certain ones disappeared in the shifting sands of historical trends, while others simply got lost in the crowd. After all, there are an awful lot of saints.

Regardless, all of them are irreplaceable tiles in the mosaic of our faith and that captivating icon of Christ. This is why we should remember them: They play important parts in your story, my story, our story. And the better we know them, the more inspired we will be to emulate them.

So read on. You'll be glad these heroic Christians are holy unknowns no more.

Sts. Perpetua and Felicity
Mothers and Martyrs
d. March 7, 203 • Pre-Congregation • Memorial: March 7

When we use Eucharistic Prayer I at Mass, we ask God for the ability to emulate a litany of saints. Sure, we recognize the apostles' names, but the others are less certain: Cosmas and Damian, Cyprian, Cornelius, Chrysogonus, Alexander, Marcellinus, and so on. Father invokes their names, but who were these people?

Two of them were Felicity and Perpetua, North African women martyred very early in the third century. While their story isn't conventionally exciting, their quiet confidence and trust in Christ and their steadfastness in their faith can teach us much about living a Christian life today.

The *Acta* (or Acts) of St. Perpetua tell us that she was a twenty-two-year-old, well-born, well-educated mother of an infant who lived in the Roman province of Africa, in the city of Carthage, which today is near Tunisia's capital.[1] St. Felicity was a pregnant slave who, along with Perpetua and four others, was rounded up in the persecutions of Emperor Septimius Severus (193–211). We know so much about these two remarkably brave women because Perpetua kept a diary of their imprisonment and trial. Hers is the oldest surviving writing by a Christian woman.

Today we have the impression that persecution under the Roman emperors was unremitting. In reality, though, it waxed and waned—sometimes it was terrible, sometimes not so bad, sometimes hardly evident at all. Life had been quiet for Carthage's Christians for several years. Around 197, however, Severus decreed that no imperial citizen could convert to Judaism or Christianity. This affected only recent converts and catechumens, which explains why Perpetua's mother and brother, both longtime Christians, were not arrested.

1

Because she was still a catechumen, however, authorities eventually arrested Perpetua, separating her from her son, who had not yet been weaned. Some deacons bribed a jailer to allow Perpetua's mother to bring her toddler to her, and she kept and nursed him for the remainder of her imprisonment. "Straightway," Perpetua wrote, in words at which many mothers will smile, "I became well and was lightened of my labour and care for the child; and suddenly the prison was made a palace for me."[2]

The palace would be short-lived, however. Perpetua had a vision of a dragon's head, bronze ladders, and beautiful vistas. She interpreted this to mean that she and the others would soon receive martyrdom.

Her pagan father didn't need a vision to understand this. He tried every means possible to get his little girl to apostatize—that is, to renounce the faith. He cried, he begged, he beseeched, he yelled, he manipulated. Perpetua simply held her ground. The two obviously loved one another, and their discord must have been hard on the saint.

At the trial the procurator, Hilarianus, got right to the point: Apostatize, or die. The soldiers then let Perpetua's father into the court, and in his arms he held her son. For the sake of your child, he admonished her, save your life. She was resolute, however. Her father became so distraught that bailiffs had to forcibly remove him.

The other Christians likewise stood firm. All were found guilty and sentenced to die while fighting beasts at games held in honor of the birthday of Septimius Severus's son, Prince Geta.

After the sentencing, Perpetua had another vision. It was similar to her first: Once again the dragon, now a serpent, tried to prevent Christians from climbing the heavenly ladder. Perpetua took this to mean that she would fight not beasts but Satan himself, and that she would emerge victorious.

Felicity was now eight months pregnant. While many may find this hard to appreciate, she had more concern about being allowed martyrdom with her companions than about her impending delivery. Roman law prohibited the execution of a pregnant woman. Two days before the scheduled execution, Felicity gave birth to a daughter, whom a Christian woman adopted. Now Felicity was free to receive the martyr's crown along with the rest.

On the day of the games, the prisoners were scourged per the crowd's wishes. Then a leopard, boar, and bear were loosed on the men, and a wild bull on the women. When the beasts had savaged them, the saints gave each other the kiss of peace, and all were put to the sword.

Last to die was Perpetua. Her *Acta* states that her swordsman was new to the job. When he thrust his sword into her, he pierced her bones rather than her flesh. Seeing the bloodied woman screaming in pain but not felled by his thrust, he became unnerved and began impotently flailing his sword. Recalling her vision, this incredible woman then grabbed his arm and put the weapon to her own neck. Her *Acta* says this is the only way she would have died that day, such was her strength.

WHY STS. PERPETUA AND FELICITY DESERVE OUR ATTENTION AND DEVOTION

In Scripture, our Savior tells us we must love God even more than we love our parents or children (see Matthew 10:37). Sometimes when we read things like this, they seem abstract. It's hard to picture what this would look like in practical terms. Well, Perpetua and Felicity give us very good examples. Both women had every reason in the world to live except one: Their doing so would have meant looking back and denying Christ. No reason for living is worth that.

Lord, help us to count nothing as great as you. Help us to not "look back." If we are doing that, help us see it clearly, and help us look ahead so that we might be fit for your kingdom.

3

St. Baudile

The John the Baptist of Southern France

d. ca. 290 • Pre-Congregation • Memorial: May 20

On any number of fronts, showing one's faith in the public square is becoming an increasingly contentious issue. Faith, we're told, should be kept private. However, as many, including the pope, have noted, not only do Christians have a right to proclaim and live our faith in public ways, but it's our absolute, God-given duty to do so. Maybe efforts in this regard should have St. Baudile as their patron.

Although details of his life are scant, historians have confirmed Baudile's existence. He came from Gaul, which we now call France, and converted to Christianity while serving in the Gallo-Roman armies. At some point Baudile became a deacon. During the reign of Diocletian (284–305), the most murderous period for Christians in Roman history, Baudile and his wife decided to move to and evangelize Nîmes. Maybe the two liked a challenge. The city had proven particularly resistant to evangelization.

One day as Baudile was walking in an oak forest just outside the city walls, he saw a pagan crowd. They were about to sacrifice to Veiovis, whom Romans regarded as one of the first gods. He was invoked for healing, so each May 21 his followers would sacrifice a female goat, hoping to prevent the outbreak of any plagues.

Seeing Baudile, the crowd asked among themselves who this stranger was, and someone recognized him as a Christian. The pagans called him over and urged him to sacrifice to the god. "Never!" he shouted at the top of his lungs, adding that their beliefs were mere superstition if not outright devil worship. His call for them to repent of their blasphemy and come to Christ is reminiscent of St. John the Baptist.

Baudile's words excited the crowd's wrath, and they menacingly pressed in on him. He was not intimidated. To add an exclamation point to his prophetic words, he took their pagan idol, held it above his head, and flung it to the ground, converting it to rubble. The now rabidly infuriated pagan priests had Baudile beaten and whipped. They then substituted him for the goat by cutting his head off with an ax. His head bounced three times before coming to a stop, and at each place a spring burst forth.

That night his wife took his corpse and buried it at Valsainte. A whole cemetery grew up around his tomb because of all the people who wanted their sepulchers near his. Whereas Nîmes had previously proven resistant to Christianity, Baudile's story inspired many conversions. Pilgrims started coming, which led to the building of first a church and then a monastery.

Devotion to the saint reached its high-water mark in the Middle Ages, just before the Renaissance. By 1685, however, the monastery and church dedicated to his patronage were completely ruined. By the early nineteenth century, devotion to his memory was a purely local phenomenon, and so it has remained to this day.

Why St. Baudile deserves our attention and devotion

Until the Berlin Wall fell in 1989, one of many things distinguishing the West from the communist East was the protection of religious freedoms and the right to act according to one's conscience. Now we see serious attempts in what we have always believed were free Western countries to curtail those freedoms, particularly where it comes to expressing our faith in the public square. When confronted by those who tell us to keep our faith private, remember St. Baudile's courageous example, and do not be intimidated.

Through St. Baudile's prayers, dear God, help us have the courage, tenacity, and love needed to show the world our faith, never in an obnoxious way but never shrinking through reticence or fear either. In this way let us be salt and light (Matthew 5:13–16).

St. Faith of Conques

The Practical Joker

ca. late third to early fourth century • Pre-Congregation

Memorial: October 6

Read the accounts of the early Christian martyrs, and one type of story comes up again and again: A twelve- to fourteen-year-old girl gets arrested during a persecution, is told to renounce her faith, refuses, and is tortured but refuses to apostatize. One thinks of Sts. Lucy, Eulalia, Agatha, Agnes, and too many others to count. It seems every region Rome ruled during this time has its own martyr whose tale follows this basic path. Some stand out, however. Consider Lucy and her eyes or Agnes and her miraculously growing hair. Or even the more obscure St. Faith of Conques.

She was a beautiful twelve-year-old girl living in Agen, Aquitaine, France, during the coreign of Diocletian and Maximian. Her parents, wealthy pagans, left her rearing to a nurse, who happened to be Christian. Growing up in a beautiful, mosaic-encrusted villa, Faith had everything the world could offer, and from her parents' perspective her future looked bright, except for one thing: She had accepted her nurse's Christian faith.

To understand why this was a problem, we must understand Emperor Diocletian. On assuming office, he had announced his intention to revive morality within the realm, since immorality was sapping Roman virtue and therefore the empire's viability and strength. He also believed a revival of the traditional Roman gods was key, because an empire united in its religious praxis would be stronger. This was not a problem for most pagans in most places, because gods were gods, even if their names varied by region. This was obviously not the case for Christians, however.

Diocletian launched a persecution designed to force everyone to the same cult. Dacian, prefect of the province in which Faith lived, came to Agen to observe his subjects' loyalty—that is, to see if they were being good pagans and, if not, to kill them.

While many Christians panicked, Faith voluntarily surrendered to the authorities. Imagine how frightened she must have been. She likely prayed for strength and for the words to convert her persecutors. Dacian probably had some nervousness too. After all, putting a twelve-year-old girl on trial would be a touchy situation, especially for a capital crime. Who wants to execute a child? Better to get her to apostatize, but how?

During the trial Faith gave a brave, remarkable defense of Christianity. Fine, Dacian told her, keep your beliefs. Just sacrifice to the goddess Diana in the town temple.

Faith refused, and Dacian lost patience with the girl. He ordered her bound naked to a brazier and roasted. Pitch was thrown on the fire to make its flames flare and burn her legs. This happened in public so that the crowds could witness the fate awaiting Christians.

The problem for Dacian was that little Faith refused to cooperate. She cried, yes, but she didn't scream or beg for mercy. After a miraculous rainstorm extinguished the flames, Dacian had her beheaded.

Seeing all this, the mob was moved not to contempt for Christianity but to pity for Faith. Their only contempt was for Dacian, the child executioner. They wondered what god of theirs could have given a mere maiden such strength. Realizing the answer was "None," many converted on the spot. In turn, most of these received martyrdom twenty days later.

After her death St. Faith developed a reputation as something of a practical joker. If someone was stingy with a donation left for her shrine's upkeep, small misfortunes might befall them. For instance, a dying woman promised St. Faith she would will her most precious ring to the abbey. Afterward her husband—possibly for its sentimental value, or maybe the thing had cost him a good deal of money—thought better of his wife's last pledge. He instead used the ring as his second wife's wedding band. Shortly the ring finger of the new missus swelled so much that it became unbearably painful. The couple beat a hasty path to the shrine. There, when the lady blew her nose, the ring flew off her hand with such force that it left a crack in the pavement.

On another occasion, Faith's prayers restored sight to a man named Guibert, whose eyes had been torn from their sockets. Wanting to keep the recipient of so great a miracle close, the monks who cared for St. Faith's shrine gave him the job of selling candles. It seems Guibert was a good businessman and soon became quite rich. But as so often happens, when financial success came, devotion to Our Lord went.

St. Faith reproached Guibert for his ingratitude. She had prayed Jesus would restore his sight, and this is how Guibert repaid her? So Guibert lost sight in one eye. This happened repeatedly: He would mend his ways, gain his eye, grow successful again, fall into sin, lose the eye, and so on.

A modern-day monk relates how the monks will occasionally parade Faith's relics around the monastery grounds. With the greatest pomp, they process while holding candles, and they sing all day. By evening they are exhausted and famished. The monk says that once when many people had prayed, the intercession of St. Faith wrought many miracles. With each miracle the monks would sing a *Te Deum*. At the end of the day, the monks sat down under a tree to have a picnic, but each time they were about to sink their teeth into their meager food, someone would cry, "A miracle!" and the monks would have to get up and sing again.

The reliquary holding St. Faith's skull looks incredibly lifelike, especially the eyes. They seem to look right at the observer. Maybe that is why Faith is the patroness of those with eye problems.

Thirty-eight churches in England alone are named after St. Faith. There are many more in northern Spain and southern France, and her fame spread to the Americas via the conquistadors. Indeed, at least four cities in the United States are named after her, including Santa Fe, New Mexico. And in Brazil alone twenty-two cities bear her name.

WHY ST. FAITH DESERVES OUR ATTENTION AND DEVOTION

Except for what she said in court, St. Faith never preached. She never wrote an epistle. Her preaching and writing were her actions. The bravery and resolve of this young maiden astounded the crowds. Perceiving something special about the God she worshiped, they converted. And she was just a child. God makes up for what we lack.

Holy Spirit, through your ineffable gifts, draw us to constant conversion. Renew our hearts. Let our actions preach eloquent sermons that draw people to Christ far better than our poor words can. Help us to love you, God, to do everything for you, and to remain firm in that love come what may, so that, with St. Faith, we may wear an eternal crown.

St. Paul of Thebes

The First Hermit

ca. 228–ca. 341 • Pre-Congregation

Memorial: January 15

Let's be honest: Many of us find prayer, well, boring. We get distracted. We rattle off a litany of wants and needs. We pray for certain people. "Thanks, God, for X, Y, Z." Make the Sign of the Cross. There. Finished. Wasn't that exciting?

Prayer, however, really can be stimulating. Each of us has the capacity to talk with God in a way that is transporting. When you have that, the world pretty quickly loses its allure. And some people are so good at prayer that they renounce a normal life. That's what happened to St. Paul of Thebes, the first Christian hermit.

In the beginning Paul practiced his faith but wasn't particularly religious. When he was sixteen his father died, and Paul and his older sister inherited the family fortune. His brother-in-law, Peter, wanted two-thirds of the estate, leaving Paul one-third. Paul refused and took Peter to court.

Walking to court, Paul saw the funeral procession for a deceased rich man, a well-known sinner. This man wore only a simple linen undershirt to his grave. Paul was dumbstruck. So much for the value of money, he thought.

Paul also learned that his brother-in-law planned to turn him over to the authorities for being a Christian. This was during the persecution of Decius and Valerianus (ca. 251–253). The persecution included torture and killing. Paul had seen a man hog-tied under the blistering sun and covered in honey so that insects would slowly devour him. The Romans also had more pernicious torments designed not so much to torture the body but to kill the soul.

Then they brought to him a gorgeous harlot, physically desirable in every way, who danced and flitted around him and then started touching him. What was the lad to do to prevent lust from winning the day?

St. Jerome relates that the young man bit off the end of his tongue and spit it in the woman's face as she bent to kiss his lips. The pain overcame any pleasure she might have induced. And so, Jerome writes, his soul was saved.

Now, through the centuries, many Christians have actively desired martyrdom. Not Paul. He didn't want to die or suffer persecution of any kind, so he fled to the desert. There he found a mountain cave near a running stream and a date palm. He wove the palm's fronds into clothing, and he ate its fruit. For two decades those dates were his only food. Then a black raven began delivering a daily loaf of bread. This provision continued another fifty-five to sixty-five years.

One day St. Anthony of the Desert, who lived in the same wilderness, was humbly considering how history would know him as the first Christian hermit. That night God mentioned in a dream that an even older hermit was nearby. Upon waking, Anthony set off to find him. He traveled three days, never sure where he was headed. He simply trusted Jesus to show the way, which he did at last through a she-wolf. When Anthony arrived at Paul's cave, Paul invited him in, and a few minutes later Paul's raven brought two loaves for them.

Paul died shortly thereafter. He who had clothed himself in woven palm fronds for almost a century was wrapped in an elaborate winding sheet provided by St. Athanasius, patriarch of Alexandria. After first being buried in the desert, his relics were next taken to Alexandria, then Venice after Egypt's fall to Islamic forces, and then Hungary, where they rest today.

WHY ST. PAUL DESERVES OUR ATTENTION AND DEVOTION

After the persecutions ended, St. Paul could have left the desert, but he chose to stay because he had come to love prayer. It put him in God's joyful, peaceful, compelling presence. In short, he found heaven on earth. Paul teaches us to persevere in our devotions. If we do, prayer will eventually become more satisfying than we ever thought possible.

Lord Jesus, living in the desert was not St. Paul's dream existence. And yet this curve in the road made him phenomenally content and happy. Through his intercession, help us accept life's twists and turns. Then let us use them to glorify you.

St. Romanus of Le Mans

The Reluctant, Shy Saint

d. 385 • Pre-Congregation

Memorial: November 24

We all know people who, if you look at their lives, aren't "special." They are not Bl. Mother Teresa or some great preacher, and yet their commitment to letting Christ soak every thread in their life's fabric is no less profound. These are the quiet saints, the ones who don't get any attention. One of the best examples of them is St. Romanus of Le Mans.

Romanus was a shy homebody who would have stayed in Italy if his uncle, St. Julian, bishop of Le Mans, had not requested his assistance. God used Romanus to bless that city's people in myriad ways, including conversions, the odd resurrection, and other miracles. And like some star athletes who kneel or point heavenward after scoring, the shy young Italian always gave the credit to God.

Within short order St. Julian ordained his nephew to the priesthood and then sent him to evangelize along the Gironde River. There Romanus won even more conversions, especially among the sailors. What makes this odd is that Romanus was inarticulate and scatterbrained. However, he also was sincere. The gospel had so convicted his heart, and he spoke of it so lovingly, that after hearing him people often immediately asked for baptism.

When Uncle Julian died, Romanus would simply not leave the tomb, neither day nor night. And so when St. Thuribe was elected Julian's successor, he asked Romanus to be the tomb's caretaker. In time Thuribe too died, and Romanus watched over his grave as well. Because the early Christians desired to be buried near the saints, a cemetery began to mushroom around the sepulchers of these two saints, and Romanus became a member of a minor order called the Fossors (Gravediggers). When Christians died, these brothers performed services not unlike those of undertakers today. They also tended tombs and ministered to the bereaved.

When he perceived that his own race had run its course, Romanus asked Bishop Pavace leave to go to Rome. The bishop gave it on the condition he come back, which he did. Romanus died shortly thereafter. For centuries his tomb was the site of significant pilgrimages, until, like a photograph left too long in the sun, remembrance of him faded.

Why St. Romanus of Le Mans deserves our attention and devotion

Sanctity comes from one thing and one thing only: Uncompromising love for God over ourselves and for his will over our own. Our Savior taught us to show that love through our treatment of others. This consists not only in easing their burdens but also in loving them so much that we try to bring them to Christ. St. Romanus is a great example of how to do both very well.

Dearest God, you call us to make disciples. By St. Romanus's prayers, daily help us discover ways to imitate his example, so that our love will bring many into your kingdom.

Sts. David and Winefride
Saints of Wales

When Great Britain was Catholic, it carried the nickname Our Lady's Dowry, and one could make a compelling argument that it was the most Catholic of all the kingdoms on earth. Devotion was particularly strong in Wales. There are parts of that country, as well as the Scottish Highlands, that remained Catholic long after the rest of the nation had cloaked itself in Protestantism's mantle. And it was people such as Sts. David and Winefride whose lasting impact made this possible.

St. David
ca. 500–March 1, 589 • Canonized: 1120
Memorial: March 1

St. David's mother was a nun, St. Non, who unwillingly became pregnant by the violence of Sandde ab Ceredig, prince of Keretica (Cardiganshire). On the run from Sandde, she gave birth to David all alone one dark night, atop a cliff during a pelting, prolonged thunderstorm. It was said the pain was so intense that she gouged the rocks there with her fingernails.

As a youth David studied for the priesthood under St. Paulinus of Wales, whose blindness David cured by making the Sign of the Cross over his eyes. After receiving holy orders, Fr. David, a uniquely gifted evangelist, traveled throughout Wales and southwest England, converting people, healing them, and founding churches and monasteries. He became abbot at one monastery, and in that capacity he attended a synod of bishops, which attracted a great crowd. The bishops had called the council to debate Pelagianism, the heresy that says good works alone can earn us salvation. David argued the orthodox position well, contributing to Pelagianism's demise. As a result, the other bishops elected him primate of Wales.

Not long afterward, our saint went on pilgrimage to Jerusalem, where that city's Latin patriarch confirmed him as archbishop of Wales. On his return to his homeland, he helped the Welsh win a battle against the invading Saxons by having each soldier wear a leek in his hat, thus helping the men distinguish ally from foe. To this day Welsh wear leeks on his feast.

After David's canonization by Pope Callixtus II in 1120, the Holy See decreed that, with respect to indulgences, two pilgrimages made to his tomb equaled one to Rome.

St. Winefride

ca. 600–November 3, 660 • Pre-Congregation
Memorial: November 3

St. Winefride was born to a wealthy father and the sister of St. Beuno. Beuno was looking for a location in which to found a monastery, and while visiting his sister and brother-in-law he noticed a lovely hill overlooking the sea. He knew he had found the place. Each day he said Mass at the chapel he built there, and each day his fifteen-year-old niece Winefride attended. She loved his sermons because they inspired in her greater devotion and piety, and she soon began spending whole nights praying before the Blessed Sacrament.

Winefride was bright, bubbly, and pretty. What made her even more attractive was her sincere piety and love for Jesus. With her parents' permission, she decided to enter a convent. However, word got around about her, and soon Caradog, son of a local prince, began observing Winefride and decided to seek her hand in marriage. He arrived one Sunday morning to make his case with her parents, but they had left for Mass. Winefride herself was just about to leave when Caradog darkened her door.

He explained why he had come, and she explained that her plans precluded matrimony. Caradog took this as a challenge, and he began pressing his case with greater and greater passion. Winefride showed him her back in disgust. Enraged at this, the sociopath lunged for her. Winefride sped from the house and ran toward the church, where Mass had already begun. Caradog gave angry pursuit, and drawing his sword as he caught her on the steep hill leading up to the church, he severed her head. It rolled down the hill, and a spring burst forth where it stopped.

Winefride's screams had drawn everyone from the church outside. On reaching his beloved niece's head, Beuno took it and put it to her neck, covered her body with his cloak, and went back to finish Mass.

After Mass, Beuno returned to his niece's corpse, removed the cloak, and saw that the head had somehow become reattached to the body. Only a thin white line gave any indication of the violence so recently committed. Winefride blinked her eyes and rose—hence her nickname, "the Welsh Lazarus." The first thing she beheld was Caradog's arrogant, smug smirk.

His ire raised, St. Beuno called down God's wrath on Caradog, which it seems the Almighty was all too willing to provide. Like a starving man offered a sumptuous feast, the ground opened up and swallowed the criminal whole.

Her father subsequently built Winefride a convent, and she became its abbess. Later a chapel was erected over the still-flowing spring. A town now called Holywell grew around it, thanks to the legions of pilgrims who have come over the ages. The well is called the Lourdes of Wales, and healings still take place there.

When the Saxons invaded Wales, Winefride and her nuns were forced to leave their convent. Like many other refugees, they made for the Welsh mountains. Thre they found refuge at a convent run by her aunt, and it was here Winefride died.

Even after her second death, Winefride's spring at Holywell continued to be a pilgrimage site. Welsh recusants made it a place of national pride in defiance of the English crown and Queen Elizabeth. At a time when being Catholic carried huge financial and criminal penalties, more than fourteen thousand pilgrims went there on her feast in 1629.

WHY STS. DAVID AND WINEFRIDE DESERVE OUR ATTENTION AND DEVOTION

In every age Christians have the duty of building the Church. This isn't easy. It doesn't allow for halfhearted devotion. Sts. David and Winefride gave their total dedication to the gospel, and we can imitate them in that, regardless of our vocation or state in life. If the only "monastery" we create is our children, let's personally teach them to love Christ and his Church. If we do, the faith in our families will be a living water, another Holywell to last throughout generations.

Lord, forgive us. Total commitment to you seems impossible. Our heads get constantly turned by this, that, and the other thing. So many distractions. No silence. You speak. We don't hear you.

Help us, then, to devote ourselves to you as Sts. David and Winefride did. Help us and our children to become "living stones," so that the edifice of your Church built on the rock of Peter may ever endure.

St. Radegund

"Not Tonight, Honey, You Killed My Brother"

518–August 13, 586 • Pre-Congregation • Memorial: August 13

No big news here: Suffering is a part of life, it affects everyone, and it won us redemption from our sins. And as many passages in St. Paul's epistles make clear, it even gives us the opportunity to cooperate with Christ's salvific work on the cross. That doesn't mean, however, that we have to grin and bear it if we find ourselves in an abusive situation such as St. Radegund did.

She was the daughter of King Berthar, who shared with his two brothers the throne of Thuringia, which is now part of north central Germany. One brother, Hermanfrid, killed Berthar and, with the help of the Merovingian king Theuderic, defeated the other in battle. When Hermanfrid broke his promise to share power with Theuderic, the latter invaded with his brother Clotaire I in 531, defeating Hermanfrid and thoroughly destroying the land. The invaders killed legions of people. Only four royals survived, including Radegund, her brother, and a cousin. Clotaire took Radegund and her brother to live at his court, where he saw to their education.

Imagine being this young girl. First she saw her father killed, and then her other relations were massacred before her eyes, and the murderer took her roughly 460 miles from home to Soissons, France, where the language, religious practice, and customs differed greatly from those of her homeland. The traumatized child became quiet and reserved. She never felt joy. She never played.

Owing to the stupid brutality she had witnessed, Radegund recognized the vanity of the desperate grasping after wealth and power, the vice that animated Clotaire's court. She may have been the one person in that palace for whom material possessions held little worth. She did, however, value knowledge, so she applied herself to her studies and soon was a master student.

19

Clotaire, nominally Christian, was the son of St. Clotilda and King Clovis, the monarchs who brought Christianity to France. Some twenty years Radegund's senior, he already had one wife and several mistresses. Nevertheless, he took one look at Radegund and decided she was his. Marrying her would also justify his claim to rule Thuringia.

Radegund likely knew of his interest, if not firsthand then by how people talked and how Clotaire looked at her. The prospect of marrying the man who had caused her so much misery did not send her heart soaring with dreams of wedded bliss. She told the few people with whom she was close that any fate would be better than marrying him.

Yet five years later, when she turned eighteen, courtiers informed her of the impending wedding date. Desperate to avoid this, she stole out of the castle to the nearby river Somme and attempted to make her escape by boat. However, she was soon caught and forced to marry Clotaire.

For ten years Radegund was a dutiful wife, but to say that she did not dote on her husband would be putting it mildly. For instance, she would make him cool his heels when he called for her, for usually it was during her prayers and daily spiritual reading and meditation. Or upon entering his chambers at night, she would immediately excuse herself to the bathroom and stay there meditating on Christ's Passion. The king her lord could wait; God her King and Lord couldn't. Maybe she hoped he would have fallen asleep by the time she finished. In any event the "couple" had no children.

What really irked Clotaire was Radegund's public behavior. She often kept him waiting at dinner, and when she did show up it was not in the fine clothes her regal position demanded but in simple clothes that helped her keep her Christian humility. She usually ate only lentils or beans, and she wore a hair shirt under her royal gowns. She kept up her learning of theology, read Scripture and other works, and queried the court clergy, and so her zeal for the Lord grew by great strides.

This exasperated Clotaire and led him once to exlaim that he was married more to a nun than to a queen. He couldn't understand. Hadn't he been good to her—clothed her in fine garments, fed her the best food, given her the best education?

Clotaire would beat Radegund and yell at her, and she would apologize, as abused wives tend to do. She knew he loved material wealth more than anything, so she would give him some present, and this, the only music he could hear, would calm his savage heart. Meanwhile, to whomever would listen, she pined about how much she longed to be a nun.

When Radegund wasn't using her wealth to placate Clotaire, she used it to aid the poor and tend the sick. If Clotaire condemned someone to death, she would move heaven and earth to save that man. She also used her power to promote the one true faith. For instance, once while passing a village's pagan shrine, she had her retinue destroy it.

Since the time she was wrenched from her homeland, Radegund's most cherished companion and closest confidant was her brother. Just as she had blossomed into the very model of womanhood, so her brother had become a fine young man. And if there was one thing the sons of Clovis and Clotilda could not abide, it was good men who might someday threaten their thrones. This is why they brutally killed two nephews right in front of their sainted mother. Clotaire feared Radegund's brother would become a leader in the Thuringian independence movement. Thus, in the eleventh year of their marriage, he had the man assassinated.

Until this happened, Radegund could tolerate her husband; now he made her skin crawl. She left him and went to her friend Bishop St. Medard of Noyon, demanding that he immediately consecrate her to the Lord. Some nobles there threatened harm to the bishop if he had any part in their queen becoming a mere nun. Fearful, Medard hesitated.

The ever-resolute Radegund turned on her heels, marched into the sacristy, found the vestment of a deaconess, dressed herself in it, went back out into the church, and knelt before the bishop. She then asked whom he feared more: these men, who could take only his life, or God, who would determine the everlasting disposition of his soul? Medard consecrated her to the Lord as a deaconess then and there, which according to feminist historian Line Eckenstein, simply meant she had the Church's protection.[1] Thereafter she went about giving her jewels and royal robes to various charitable causes.

Her husband previously gave her some lands around Poitiers, where she built her monastery, Holy Cross. Its charism was to serve lepers, mental patients, and other sick people, and it grew into one of the first hospitals in France.

Even before the abbey was built, however, Clotaire decided he wanted Radegund back. Learning of this, she fled to the tomb of St. Hilary of Poitiers and claimed sanctuary. Upon discovering her location, Clotaire burst into the church and marched up the aisle to the saint's sepulcher. Seeing his wife there vested as a nun, that icy stare speaking without words the coldness toward him that permeated every fiber of her heart, the very presence of God in this place of St. Hilary's burial, all combined to thwart his pride and stubbornness. He left her unmolested to complete her work, and the abbey church was consecrated in 550.

With the monastery finished, Radegund became a regular nun, giving the role of abbess to Sr. Agnes, a fellow noble. Through royal connections Radegund obtained from Constantinople various relics, including a piece of the true cross. When these arrived in 559, her best friend, Fortunatus, composed the *Vexilla Regis* and *Pange Lingua*, which Catholics still sing to this day.

These relics drew pilgrims from around Europe. Even with all these people around, Radegund, as she made clear in her two surviving poems, always felt the loneliness that had been hers since being taken from her homeland.

Clotaire decided once more to win her back. Radegund, however, must have had good spies, and she begged St. Germain of Paris to convince the king to leave her alone. Meeting His Majesty before St. Martin's tomb at Tours, Germain begged him to reconsider. Finally the man showed some hint of repentance. He fell to his knees and told Germain to tell Radegund that if she would forgive and pray for him, he would never bother her again.

She took him at his word and began praying for his conversion, which by the time he became sole king of France, after his brother's death, had largely happened. At this point material possessions and power failed to excite him much. He made a general confession to a priest at St. Martin's tomb and began to endow many monasteries and churches. Sadly, it wasn't all sweetness and light. When one of his sons revolted, he had the young man, his wife, and their little children boarded up in their home. Clotaire then ordered the place to be torched until only glowing embers remained.

It says something about how well-loved Radegund was by her four remaining stepsons that they gave her financial support and that she never fell out of favor with any of them, even though each was constantly at war with the others after their father's death. They even went to her for arbitration if they had disputes they were willing to have mediated. Furthermore, two of the stepsons' wives, Queen Frédégonde and Queen Brunhilde, loved her, although they absolutely despised each other. It is little wonder that contemporaries considered Radegund head and shoulders above not only other women but even most men—high praise indeed, when we consider the times.

Radegund died in 586, and since the nuns of her community were strictly cloistered they could not attend her funeral outside the convent walls. And so they stood on those walls to watch as her coffin processed, mourning in a way that must have broken the heart. After her burial, pilgrims flocked to her tomb, and it became the site of many miracles. Over the centuries the tomb became lost, but when it was rediscovered in 1562 the Calvinists took Radegund's bones, burned them, and scattered the remains.

WHY ST. RADEGUND DESERVES OUR ATTENTION AND DEVOTION:
"Offer up your sufferings" does not mean "Be a milquetoast," and St. Radegund gives us an inspiring example of this. Indeed, for her bravery, strength, integrity, and humility—and for counting Christ above all else—she is a great model for us all.

Lord Jesus, we unite our sufferings with your cross in repentance for our sins, the liberation of the holy souls in purgatory, and the salvation of sinners. Through the prayers of your servant Radegund, let us boldly live for you, happily leaving the results entirely to your discretion.

St. Gontram

The Other "Good King"

ca. 532–March 28, 592 • Pre-Congregation

Memorial: March 28

Even a cursory glance at the headlines suffices to show that our world hungers for good leaders, especially Catholics who let their faith vividly color their work in the public square. Good King St. Gontram did just this and, though he stumbled often, he never gave up trying to become a better Christian.

The grandson of Clovis and St. Cunigunde, Gontram was the second son of King Clotaire I and a stepson of St. Radegund. He became king of Orleans and Burgundy at age sixteen upon his father's death.

Gontram sure didn't start off a saint. He had many premarital relations, fathering several children out of wedlock. When he did marry, he was unfaithful to his wife, Marcatrude, and later he divorced her. Of course, this may have had something to do with her poisoning his oldest son, who had been born of a concubine whom Marcatrude hated.

After his divorce Gontram married the slave Austrechilde. Marcatrude's brothers were outraged the king would replace their sister with someone of such low estate. They pledged that any children Gontram had by Austrechilde would never claim the throne. Infuriated, Gontram stabbed both brothers and confiscated their considerable lands and fortunes.

Then an amazing thing happened: We know not why, but His Majesty had a complete transformation. He generously helped the poor, who took to calling him "Good King Gontram," and personally cared for the sick. When plagues broke out, he coordinated relief efforts and planned special liturgies as well. He was merciful, merely throwing into prison rather than executing two men sent by his sister-in-law Queen Frédégonde on different occasions to assassinate him. Keep in mind that once, when she had nowhere else to turn, this woman had begged

Gontram's protection for herself and her son, and he had given it. On the personal side, he spent hours fasting, praying, and weeping in sorrow for his sins.

During the early part of his reign, he had to frequently take up arms, sometimes against the Arian Lombards but usually against his own brothers. Yet unlike his brothers, Gontram never attacked someone first. He also severely punished wayward officers and any soldier guilty of pillaging or licentiousness, but he readily forgave the perpetrator if the man showed contrition.

Even after his conversion, though, Gontram did some very unsaintly things, which is to say he was not immune to his family's bad qualities. When his brother was excommunicated, for instance, Gontram invited this man's wife to stay at his palace. On her arrival, he not only confiscated all her wealth but insinuated that she was untrustworthy and unable to satisfy his brother in the way of spouses. When she attempted escape, he had her beaten and thrown in a cell.

When even the whiff of a rumor reached Gontram that his life was in danger, his paranoia knew no bounds. Coming from that family, though, that seems perfectly understandable. His father, Clotaire I, stabbed his two nephews so he could take the kingdoms they would have inherited as adults. It was common for his relatives to either start civil wars or send assassins to kill each other, often in horrifying ways.

So we can understand his paranoia. However, Gontram let his fears get the better of him and tortured men into confession. He also went about with a security detachment that would have made the Secret Service look careless. Indeed, his paranoia was so great that historians record that he actually stood up during Mass once and said, in effect, "Please don't kill me during Mass. In fact, let me live long enough to rear my orphaned nephews. And even when they're grown, keep in mind that if you murder me, you will no longer have any man of sufficient strength to defend the realm. So, again, to repeat, please don't kill me during

Mass, and, remember, it's a bad idea regardless. Trust me. Now just so we're all clear on this, no murdering me during Mass, right?"

Still, for all his faults Gontram was far above any contemporary monarch who called himself a Christian. During one rage he demanded the execution of a servant but deeply grieved his actions afterward. When he castigated Austrasian rebel envoys, they threatened him with death. Instead of killing them, he merely had them bombarded with fresh feces and thrown out. One biographer cites this as evidence of his Christian magnanimity.

Another thing that made Gontram different was his refusal to accept a bribe to fill a bishop's see. Additionally, he concerned himself with the morality of his people, enacting laws against incestuous marriages and increasing penalties for sexually related crimes. Per the third commandment, Gontram told bishops to keep Sundays holy, and he led by example, making the Sabbath a day of total rest. He also fully supported the Church's evangelization efforts. He did all of this because he understood that a moral people more easily governs itself and so is more easily governed.

Gontram thus sought to follow gospel precepts, and his reign was both prosperous and relatively peaceful. St. Gregory the Great of Tours believed God had made of Gontram a Christian King Hezekiah, the Judean monarch of the eighth century BC who restored orthodox Jewish worship after years of idolatry. Gontram died in his bed on March 28, 592.

WHY ST. GONTRAM DESERVES OUR ATTENTION AND DEVOTION

St. Gontram shows that politics and the gospel are not opposed. Indeed, politics is at its best when the teachings of Christ and his Church animate a vision of the common good.

Gontram fell again and again, often in big ways, but he kept repenting and learning from his mistakes. He didn't quit, and he became a saint.

Dear Lord, in an age with such weak leadership, where the greatest sin, it seems, is to admit to being a committed, convinced, faithful Christian, help leaders to learn from and profit by St. Gontram's example. Help also those whose family lives are difficult. Through his intercession, bring reconciliation. We humbly ask this, Christ our King, in your name.

St. Deicolus of Lure

A Tree in Autumn Can Still Bear Fruit

ca. 530–January 18, 625 • Pre-Congregation

Memorial: January 18

Circumstances permitting, we expect the elderly to retire and rest on their laurels. After all, they have worked hard for decades; now they should enjoy the rewards of their labors. We certainly don't expect them to bear much fruit during this period in their lives. After all, these are called the autumn years, and not much grows in autumn. However, as St. Deicolus of Lure shows us, this isn't always the case.

Deicolus was born in Ireland, and while a monk there he met and became an early disciple of St. Columban. When this great monastic discerned God's call to win souls for Jesus in continental Europe, Deicolus and his brother St. Gall were among the twelve men chosen to accompany him.

In 576 they arrived in Gaul, modern-day France, and Columban established his base at Luxeuil. The work was hard, but St. Deicolus did whatever his abbot asked of him in the service of the gospel. People everywhere felt attracted to the monks' humility, kindness, and charity, like moths to a flame. Another thing that attracted so many to these men was how simply they lived. They subsisted on herbs, vegetables, wild berries, and even tree bark. All in all, their behavior stood in stark contrast to the barbarians who routinely made raids, the noblemen who pretended at Christianity but were pagan at heart, and many clergy who edified few by their behavior.

Soon huge crowds were flocking to Luxeuil and another monastery Columban established. In fact, so many aspirants came that the monks had to build a third abbey. For twenty years life was good.

But it was too good for some. The local bishops grew jealous of Columban's popularity and growing influence, although this alone probably wouldn't have hurt him too badly. What really caused Columban trouble was his John the Baptist–like efforts against royal vice.

King Theuderic II of Burgundy was under the firmly pressed thumb of his grandmother Brunhilde, who encouraged him toward licentiousness. She feared that if he married, his queen would either diminish or usurp her power. Theuderic needed little encouragement, and he sired four sons by as many women. At the same time he deeply admired Columban, so the saint tried to coax him into a moral lifestyle. This threatened Brunhilde, who stoked the bishops' resentment of the abbot. In 610, Theuderic sentenced Columban to prison.

Although he was in his eighties and older than Columban, Deicolus resolved that, as he had followed Columban this far, he would not leave him now. Walking with him to jail, however, the old man lasted just twelve miles. His age and infirmities prevented him from going any farther. He asked Columban to release him to finish out his years there in the woods.

Columban didn't want to leave the old man. This was his oldest and most faithful companion. But he couldn't carry him. Furthermore, given the political situation, he couldn't stay with him. Recognizing this as God's inscrutable will, Columban sadly bid his countryman *Slán a fhágáil ag duine,* "Good-bye." And blessing one another, they parted, never to see one another again this side of heaven.

St. Columban had once asked Deicolus, "How does it happen that your face is always shining with joy and nothing seems to trouble your soul?"

"Because," Deicolus said, "nothing can ever part me from my God."[1]

Now it was just God and him, alone in the forest, and a marshy, carnivore- and mosquito-filled forest at that. Deicolus had to find shelter. Farther and farther into the woods he went, sweltering in the heat. But at sundown he hadn't found a suitable place to settle.

The next morning, faint from thirst, he knelt in prayer, asking God to do for him what he had done for Moses in the desert. Filled with faith, Deicolus rose and struck the ground with his walking staff, and water bubbled up, allowing him to drink. Refreshed, he traveled until he came upon a pasture. There he found a herd of swine feeding themselves. The swineherd was shocked to see another person in such a remote place and someone so aged besides, wearing what was to him strange garb. Was this a bandit?

Putting the man at ease, Deicolus asked where he should establish his home. The herdsman suggested the nearby wilderness called Lure, since it had water. When Deicolus asked him to show the way, the man demurred. He couldn't leave his animals. Deicolus plunged his staff into the ground, assuring his new friend it would guard the pigs in his absence. After taking the saint to his new home and helping him set up his tent, the swineherd returned and found his swine close to the staff.

Not long after Deicolus had built himself a more suitable home, King Clotaire II—cousin of Theuderic and great-grandson of St. Clotilde and King Clovis—was out hunting boar nearby. Fleeing Clotaire's hounds, one large porcine specimen sought refuge in the monk's cell, hiding behind the saint. Deicolus patted the wild pig on his head and, smiling, said, "Since thou hast sought charity here, thou shalt find safety also."[2]

Out stepped Deicolus onto his stoop. The king's dogs were in full pursuit of the beast, but they skidded to a stop short of the door. It was as if they dared go no further.

When Clotaire arrived, the scene intrigued him. Who was this aged man living alone in the woods? On learning of Deicolus's relation to Columban, whom the king loved, His Highness began talking with our saint, and Clotaire left awed by the man's sanctity. Shortly thereafter he gave Deicolus all the land around Lure as well as the town of Bredana, its church, and a nearby vineyard.

Now, the pastor didn't think much of the king's gift. Each night the priest made a show of territoriality by locking the church doors, and each night angels would open them for Deicolus. The curate accused him of sorcery and called him an itinerant monk.

The parishioners, however, sensed something else about this strange old fellow. In the spirit of Gamaliel, they counseled Father that if this man's work wasn't of God, it would soon become painfully evident (see Acts 5:33–39). They would see to that. However, if it was of God, they had no right to stand in his way.

Sadly, the more the monk's holiness became evident, the more the pastor became jealous and spiteful. Finally he encircled the entire church with large branches from nearby thornbushes. No matter. The next morning Deicolus was found praying before the Blessed Sacrament as usual.

Now this priest was *really* mad, and he asked the nefarious Count Werfarius to have Deicolus killed. The count agreed. However, immediately on giving the order, the nobleman fell dead. His widow, Berthilda, sent for the saint.

Arriving hot and tired from the journey, Deicolus took off his cloak. When a servant came to take it, he found it suspended, the story says, on a ray of sunlight. Amazed, Berthilda prostrated herself before the holy man's feet and begged forgiveness for what her husband had attempted.

Deicolus labored to complete a monastery for the many men who had joined him by this time, but the work taxed what was left of his strength. On January 18, 625, knowing he would die that day, he called for his monks. He urged them to follow the law of charity above all others and to persist in their struggle for sanctity and thus heaven, as nothing else matters. After hugging each of them, he rested his head and slept, never to reawaken in this world.

Almost twelve hundred years later, French revolutionaries would destroy Deicolus's monastery, as they did so many others. But unlike other saints whose remembrance disappeared once their shrines were destroyed, Deicolus is not completely obscure. Indeed, around Lure there are many children named after him. And the water that miraculously sprang up to quench his thirst that one hot day still flows and attracts local pilgrims. On the trees that surround the spring, parents hang their children's clothes as votive offerings for cures, since this water is especially beneficial against childhood diseases.

WHY ST. DEICOLUS DESERVES OUR ATTENTION AND DEVOTION

Society today so little values our aged, and yet St. Deicolus accomplished his greatest work in his autumn years. The reason is simple: He always worked for God's glory rather than his own. "Nothing can ever part me from my God," he said.[3]

Such beautiful, humble trust in divine providence usually comes only after much experience. Deicolus helps us see what is important and why we should value all our brothers and sisters, regardless of their age or condition. After all, look hard enough at them, and maybe we'll see Christ.

Dear Lord Jesus, through the prayers of St. Deicolus, help me follow his example of humility, perseverance in pursuing holiness, and radical reliance on your grace and providence. Also, please enable me to recognize you in all the persons whom I encounter, now and for the rest of my life.

St. Fiacre

Chauvinistic Worker of the Land

b. seventh century–d. August 18, ca. 670 • Pre-Congregation

Memorial: August 18

When we think of saints, we think of, well, people who were perfect. They didn't hold grudges or stereotype people. Well, St. Fiacre explodes that notion, but he also shows that God writes straight with crooked lines.

The son of an Irish king, Fiacre was entrusted to St. Conan for his education. Conan taught him to love our Lord and prayer. After his ordination, Fiacre went to live as a hermit in County Kilkenny. Owing to his impressive ability to heal people with herbs and homeopathic remedies to great effect, he drew huge numbers of people.

As this made living the eremitical life slightly difficult, Fiacre emigrated to Meaux, France, where he asked of Bishop St. Faro permission to establish his hermitage in a nearby forest. Irish priests were learned and Faro longed for intellectual company, so Faro readily agreed.

At first Fiacre was alone, but eventually people were once again coming to see him in droves, which he took as God's will. He eventually constructed a small chapel, a hospice, and a small, remote dwelling for himself. That travelers' hospice eventually became the town of Saint-Fiacre.

One problem was that Fiacre kept running out of room to serve the multitudes who came to him. So he went to Faro, who told him he could have as much property as he could mark out with the tip of his staff between sunup and sundown of one day. The excited Fiacre went to work with a vengeance. He madly plowed with his walking stick, uprooting trees, tossing weeds, ripping out thorny briers with his bare hands, all in an attempt to compass as much land as possible.

A woman named Becnaude saw this and thought him possessed, since he was toppling some pretty big trees. Frightened, she ran to tell Faro, and he realized she was probably describing Fiacre. Becnaude then ran back to Fiacre and, screeching like a harpy, told him he was in trouble. Her words went unheard, though, because he was daydreaming of all the wonderful things God would do through this monastery. Lost in thought, he had sat his skinny hermit self on a granite rock. This softened like wax and received the imprint of his backside.

When Faro arrived and saw the marked stone, he recognized God at work, saying, "One can doubt everything except for a Scot's rear!"[1] When Faro told him of Becnaude's report, Fiacre was incensed. He forever banished women from his monastery. If any dared come anyway, they risked a severe thrashing from him, fairer sex or no.

On his death, his followers made his tomb in Meaux's cathedral, which became a great pilgrimage site. Because of the stone incident, he is particularly invoked for relief from hemorrhoids.

WHY ST. FIACRE DESERVES OUR ATTENTION AND DEVOTION

It's hard to understand how St. Fiacre could stereotype all women and still be a saint. Then again, it's hard to understand how St. Jerome could be an irascible cuss and how St. Paul could tolerate slavery. This shows the importance of ceaselessly asking God to reveal how he sees our attitudes.

Also, give Fiacre credit. He wanted to be a hermit. By serving those who came to him, however, he sacrificed his desires for a greater good. Can we say the same?

Lord, which of my attitudes do you find appalling for someone who is called a Christian? Give me the light to see this and to serve you as you will, even if it means sacrificing my own inclinations. You are almighty and all-knowing, so I can confidently place my trust in you.

St. Bathilde

The Slave Queen

ca. 626–January 30, 680 • Canonized: ca. 880

Memorial: January 26; in France, January 30

What would you do if you suddenly won the jackpot or had unimaginable power? How would it change you? For better or for worse? What about those you know? Before you answer, consider the case of St. Bathilde.

Bathilde was an English noblewoman whom Danish Vikings kidnapped in 641. They sold her as a slave to the recently widowed Erchinoald, mayor of the palace for King Clovis II of France, a position akin in some ways to prime minister, in other ways to a president's chief of staff.

Pretty, kind, modest, and blessed with a natural charisma, Bathilde was a good servant to her master and even took pains to serve her fellow slaves. With someone so young, virtuous, and attractive in every way, it would have been surprising if Erchinoald had not wanted her as his wife. She had no such interest in him, however, and when she learned of his intent, she hid until he had married another woman.

After her return, she caught the eye of King Clovis II. Like her master, Clovis found this woman to have a whole package of appealing qualities. Unlike the forty-something master, Clovis was young. He was also handsome and a good Christian, relative to the times. So it was that Bathilde, at age nineteen, became Queen of the Franks.

The couple had three boys, and it was a good, well-matched marriage, but they lasted less than a decade, as Clovis died before 658. At his passing their eldest son, Clotaire, was just five, so Bathilde reigned as regent for eight years.

During her rule she used public monies to ransom slaves. This was at a time when taxes were so high that the only way many poor parents could pay them was to sell their children into bondage. Bathilde also reduced this tax burden and made a start on abolition by making it illegal to sell Christians or French subjects into slavery. Furthermore, she freed foreign slaves who made it into France.

Bathilde outlawed simony and supported several saintly bishops in their work. Along the way she founded several abbeys, encouraged better agriculture and thus a greater abundance of crops, and established hospitals by selling her jewelry.

Thus Bathilde was a tremendous regent, exemplifying the humble servant-monarch. She knew God had blessed her, so she dared not use riches or power for her desires. She used them to help others.

The opinion of her sanctity is not unanimous, however. For instance, the *Vita Sancti Wilfrithi* says that Bathilde was downright ruthless in retaining power and that several people, including nine bishops, were even assassinated at her command. Closer investigation, however, reveals that Ébroïn, who had replaced Erchinoald as mayor of the palace, was more likely the guilty party. Also, consider the Merovingian dynasty to which Bathilde's husband and sons belonged, the dynasty founded by Clovis and St. Clotilde. She almost certainly understood that her duty as regent was to have a throne to give her son when he came of age, no matter the cost. Christians sometimes see the gospel imperfectly, refracted as it is through each age's attitudes.

One biographer, a nun, wrote that, although Bathilde hadn't ordered the assassination of Bishop Sigobrand of Paris, he actually deserved it, for he had tried to turn her sons against her. That a nun would think anyone—let alone a bishop—deserved murder for whatever reason says a lot about the tenor of those times. In any event, Ébroïn removed Bathilde as regent, and she in turn gave her son the reins of power in 664. This marked the beginning of the end of the Merovingian dynasty.

Bathilde then took the veil at an abbey she had founded near Paris. Although probably compelled to do so by Ébroïn, Bathilde had long wanted this sort of life, and after becoming a religious she grew in sanctity by leaps and bounds. Each day she strove to progress in virtue. Each day she worked to recapture the spirit of service and humility that had attracted her husband. Maybe this is why, unlike many aristocrats who similarly left the world for the cloister, she willingly remained just a commonplace nun, always placing herself under the obedience of another, always volunteering for the most menial tasks.

On her deathbed she told those around her that she saw a ladder reaching to heaven and she would soon climb it.[1]

WHY ST. BATHILDE DESERVES OUR ATTENTION AND DEVOTION: Many see power and possessions as ends. The poor in spirit, however, realize that these things are only means. The end—that is, their ultimate goal—is to serve others. By serving others with her blessings, St. Bathilde stockpiled her treasure in heaven. This makes her a great role model not only for politicians and the wealthy but for all of us.

Lord, teach us how to use your blessings. Through the prayers and selfless example of St. Bathilde, let us use them to serve humanity and give you glory, Almighty God. And like her, may we gain for ourselves an eternal crown.

St. Odilia of Alsace

Daddy Wanted Her Dead

ca. 662–ca. 720 • Pre-Congregation

Memorial: December 13

If the butcher, baker, or candlestick maker treats us unkindly, if relations with our siblings or others go bad, we will, being adults, survive. But when our parents treat us poorly or even reject us, that wound cuts to the bone. In God, though, we have the perfect parent. He stands by us because he knows that our worth has nothing to do with our parents' treatment of us. Rather, as St. Odilia shows us, it comes from our dignity as human persons made in his image.

After Odilia's birth in Obernheim, France, her father Duke Adalric exploded with a dumbfounding rage when told his newborn was blind. Believing this handicap would bring him shame, he ordered her death. His wife, Bereswinda, argued that Odilia's infirmity might be God's will, but Adalric wouldn't listen. He wouldn't even allow the child to receive a name or be baptized. The horrified Bereswinda pleaded with her husband to let the innocent baby live. Some accounts say he refused, others that he relented so long as the baby was taken far away and no one knew of her origins. Either way, God protected Odilia, as Bereswinda took her to live with a peasant woman who knew the girl's secret.

At age twelve Odilia was sent to the local convent for her education. When the sisters learned she was unbaptized, they arranged for Bishop St. Erhard of Regensburg to perform the sacrament. God had told him in a dream to travel over two hundred miles to the convent precisely for this purpose. God had also directed him to give the girl the name Odilia, meaning "daughter of light." When Erhard touched her eyes with the baptismal chrism, she could see, just as God had told him she would.

Now, Odilia's older brother Hugh had never forgotten her. On learning she was alive, and without consulting his father, he wrote and invited her home. It was an opportune time, because some nuns had grown jealous of Odilia and wanted her gone. Hugh prepared a celebration for his sister, and at her arrival a crowd started cheering.

When Adalric learned what was happening, he gave full rein to his fury, drew his sword, and slew his son. Grieved he had done this, he welcomed his daughter home. She left again, however, when she learned he had arranged a marriage for her despite knowing she had consecrated her life to Christ.

Adalric hunted for Odilia, found her hiding in a cave, and was going to kill her but for some reason relented. Instead, he gave her a castle, where she established the convent of Odilienberg, and many came to Christ through its nuns' good works.

When Odilia died, her sisters wept and fervently prayed to have her back. God heard their prayers. Odilia revived, described heaven's greatness, took viaticum, and passed away again.

WHY ST. ODILIA DESERVES OUR ATTENTION AND DEVOTION

No parent is perfect. All will fail us at some point, which can make us question ourselves. Some, like Adalric, are horribly abusive. This comes from a disability—not a physical one but a blindness of the soul.

The pain caused by bad parenting can feel excruciating and can last a lifetime. In her understanding that it wasn't her dad's abusiveness that reflected her worth but rather her dignity as a daughter of God, and in her reliance on the perfect model of parenthood, God the Father, St. Odilia gives us all hope. God is a parent who loves, nurtures, heals. He keeps his promises.

Father God, heal our woundedness. We give you these wounds. We invite you into them. Mend and wash them with your Son's precious blood. Give us St. Odilia's strength, and through her prayers enable us to do great things for your name's sake.

St. Richard of Lucca

What Profits a Man...

ca. 670–ca. 725–726 • Pre-Congregation

Memorial: February 7

We know little about St. Richard, a pilgrim who, St. Bede says, ruled the old British kingdom of Wessex from roughly 688 to 725. He is thought to be the grandson of Queen St. Seaxburha and the brother-in-law of St. Boniface, and his name probably wasn't Richard but Hlothere. We also know he was married and had three children, all of whom became saints: Walburga, Wunibald, and Willibald.

After a thirty-seven-year reign, King Richard abdicated in order to better pursue his goal of being a saint. He took his two sons with him on pilgrimage to Rome, which St. Willibald's biography says was the boys' idea. Having made his way across Europe and through roughly a third of Italy, he stopped in Lucca. There he developed a terrible fever and died after several days.

Richard's sons had him buried in the Church of San Frediano, which also holds the incorrupt St. Zita. During the Middle Ages his tomb saw great veneration by pilgrims. Many came from Germany as well as Britain, since some of his relics had been sent to Eichstätt, where St. Willibald was bishop. Scads of miracles occurred at his tomb. Even to this day, pilgrims praying before his impressive sarcophagus know that they are in the presence of a spiritual powerhouse.

WHY ST. RICHARD DESERVES OUR ATTENTION AND DEVOTION

A man who abandoned worldly power to pursue sanctity and who raised three saints is no slouch. His devotion left an indelible impression on his offspring, and they brought many souls to Christ as a result.

Lord, help us convert our hearts. Make us ever more perfect disciples, like St. Richard. Enable us to be shining lights for those in our care, and let them carry that light into the world and thereby bring others into your everlasting embrace of love.

St. Willibrord

If at First You Don't Succeed ...

ca. 658–November 7, 739 • Pre-Congregation
Memorial: November 7

Christ told us all to make disciples (see Matthew 28:19). If that was easy, the whole world would have long ago become Christian. As St. Willibrord shows, though, we can never quit trying.

Willibrord hailed from Northumbria, that large swath of land that encompassed northern England and southeast Scotland. While our saint was still a toddler, his father, St. Wilgis, withdrew to a hermitage, later building a small chapel that became a monastery. When the boy reached school age, Wilgis sent him to Ripon Abbey. He wanted Willibrord to grow up "in a place where he could see nothing but what was virtuous and hear nothing but what was holy."[1] The father's hope was that Willibrord would be so exposed to truth, beauty, and goodness as a youth that as a man he would know how to recognize their counterfeits.

At age fifteen Willibrord became a Benedictine monk, and he remained one for five years. Hearing about the work being done for the Lord at Rath Melsigi Abbey in Ireland, he obtained his abbot's permission to move there. Many believe Europe was saved through the Christian learning preserved and spread by Irish monks. Rath Melsigi was the epicenter of this academic movement. For twelve years Willibrord studied theology and was trained as a preacher and apologist.

These arts were in high demand; Christian rulers regularly asked King Ecgberht to send evangelists to their realms. And so it was that Pepin of Héristal requested monks to convert Frisia, which today stretches from northwestern Holland to the border of Denmark. Pepin ruled Gaul (also known as Francia) and wanted to add Frisia to his realm. But he certainly didn't want the headaches of ruling a pagan land.

The recently ordained Willibrord led the mission. On the monks' arrival, the Frisian king Radbod and his people proved so hostile that the missionaries retreated to Pepin's court. There Pepin had them evangelize those of his subjects who still embraced paganism, and Willibrord met with great success. Later he evangelized Denmark with modest results.

Willibrord's dedication so impressed Pepin that he told him to go to Rome and be consecrated a bishop. The saint replied he wasn't worthy of the position. Having listed the qualities that St. Paul said a bishop must have, he detailed how he fell short in each.

Time only confirmed Pepin's opinion of Willibrord's fitness for the episcopacy, so he suggested it again. Again the saint demurred. But when even his companions unanimously echoed Pepin's judgment, he consented and made the journey to the Eternal City, where Pope St. Sergius I consecrated him a bishop.

There followed a period of almost frenetic apostolic activity, with Willibrord erecting abbeys and churches in many places throughout Frisia to serve the many souls his evangelists were now gaining for Christ. Where once he had failed, Willibrord now experienced success.

However, King Radbod resented all of this missionary activity. Whatever the monks' intent, he understood Pepin's motivation to spread Christianity was at least partly to get his foot in the Frisian door. Radbod knew if his people accepted Christ it would inexorably lead to their domination by the Franks. Rather than harassing the missionaries, however, he took his fight to Pepin, who defeated him in 689 and compelled him to cede the western half of his kingdom. Then Pepin conquered Utrecht, Frisia's largest city.

When Pepin died in 714, Radbod went on the offensive and, in two years, recaptured much of his territory. In the process he terrorized the missionaries, killing them when he could, driving them from their abbeys when he could not, and burning their churches regardless. Interestingly, Radbod once came close to converting. Just as he was about to step into the baptismal font, however, he asked Willibrord whether his ancestors were in heaven. No, Willibrord replied, since all pagans were assuredly in hell. Radbod said he would prefer to spend eternity there with his relations than in the bliss of heaven without them.

Willibrord later earned Radbod's enmity by destroying local temples and idols or using them in ways the local pagans found sacrilegious. For instance, he used the sacred well at the temple of Fosite as a baptismal font and butchered its sacred cows. St. Willibrord did this to show that these were false gods and idols that had no power against the true God, Jesus Christ.

After his death in 739, Willibrord's tomb at Echternach Abbey in Luxembourg became a popular pilgrimage destination. In our own times, every Whit (or Pentecost) Tuesday, townspeople honor him by observing the Sprangprozessioùn, a one-mile dancing procession that ends at the abbey.

WHY ST. WILLIBRORD DESERVES OUR ATTENTION AND DEVOTION

Whether we're making disciples, pastoring a parish, raising children, teaching students, or performing some other duty in life, we'll inevitably experience disappointment, even failure. We'll make mistakes. St. Willibrord teaches us to persevere. Somehow, some way, God will reward our efforts if they are done for his kingdom. As St. Padre Pio would advise many years later, "Pray, hope, and don't worry."

Dear Christ, assist our efforts for your kingdom. Clear and straighten our path. Increase our fruitfulness. When you allow obstacles or disappointment, give us hope. Remind us to persevere. More importantly, remind us that our faith must be in your awesome, almighty power, your attractiveness, and the movement of the Holy Spirit, not in our weak abilities. Help us trust that—in you, for you, with the power of your Holy Name—we can do all things.

St. Gangolf

The Cuckold

d. May 11, 760 • Pre-Congregation • Memorial: May 11

If someone in Western society either isn't from a broken family or doesn't know someone who is, it would be a miracle. There are just so many of them, and a root cause of this is often infidelity. When a spouse cheats, however, St. Gangolf proves divorce isn't the only option.

Born in the eighth century, Gangolf's parents were wealthy Christian landowners. They gave him a good, Christ-centered education that stirred in him a love for Jesus and an aversion to sin. As a teen, while peers gallivanted and mocked chastity, Gangolf focused on growing in virtue. He often went hunting, but he also spent hours reading the Bible.

When his parents died, Gangolf inherited their lands and managed them so well that he grew even wealthier. However, if the poor or some church needed money, it was theirs. Gangolf saw this as repaying God for all his blessings. Life was good.

Then our saint made a critical mistake by marrying a woman named Ganea. Lovely to behold, she was noble by birth but not by virtue. She was worldly in every sense, her soul diseased by vice.

Because he was an accomplished soldier, Gangolf often fought for King Pepin the Short. Returning from one campaign, he and his soldiers stopped to eat at a meadow in Champagne. There was a beautiful spring whose water was clear and clean, not like the cloudy creeks back at Varennes. Furthermore, varied and beautiful flowers flourished around it. Gangolf invited the property's owner to eat with them and asked the man's price for the spring. Thinking he had a fool on his hands— for who would buy a spring many leagues from his home?—the man demanded and received a hundred silver pieces

His friends laughed at Gangolf both for the price he paid and the fact that this little spring was so far away. His wife did not find it funny.

Ganea was incensed he had made such a stupid expenditure.

One evening, having invited his friends for dinner, Gangolf took them for a walk about his estate. At a certain spot he stuck his walking staff in the ground and then bid them all good night. Just after dawn he told a servant to retrieve his staff, as he had no water with which to wash. Confused, the servant did as commanded, and on returning reported that a spring of clear water had burst from that spot. Did an "I told you so" look pass from husband to wife?

On returning home from another campaign, Gangolf learned Ganea had been unfaithful. Heartbroken at the very thought, he questioned his wife, and she denied it. Gangolf took her to the spring and told her to pick up a stone at the bottom. If she told the truth, nothing would happen. If she hadn't, God would make that clear.

Smiling inwardly, Ganea agreed. She passed her arm through the cool water to grab a rock, but she quickly began screaming in pain. Her arm looked as if it had been scalded with hot water. Evidently the rumors were accurate. Ganea avoided her husband's disbelieving yet crushed gaze.

Gangolf told her he forgave her. However, he asked her to repent before they could reconcile. He would financially support her until then. Gangolf exiled her lover, however. He then moved to another of his properties, where he devoted himself to prayer and managing his estates.

For whatever reason, Gangolf's kindness hardened Ganea's heart. Creeping vines of prideful anger now fertilized with humiliation sprouted from her dark-soiled adultery, for the effect of sin is more sin. These vines produced a putrid flower of hatred for Gangolf, and the fruit of this evil growth was a plot to kill him.

Ganea called her lover back. She stoked in him embers of fear that Gangolf might seek a violent revenge. Next she sent this submissive stripling to her husband's home on a Friday night, and while the saint serenely slept, the clerk hacked at him with his sword. Somehow awakened at the last moment, Gangolf tried to defend himself. His assailant nonetheless made a decisive cut on his upper leg, and the damage was done. Gangolf lingered two days before dying.

Meanwhile the lover returned to Ganea, and they danced to celebrate Gangolf's demise. Something in the dance moved him, and he excused himself to go to the toilet. As to what happened next, suffice it to say he died the same death as Judas did (see Acts 1:18).

Gangolf's burial took place three days later at St. Peter Church, which he had built at Varennes. People began immediately reporting miracles at the tomb. When a servant girl excitedly recounted the reports to Ganea, the vexed and bitter wife retorted, "Gangolf works miracles as well as my [rear] sings songs."[1] Immediately the most shameful noise escaped from that part of this woman. Every Friday thereafter, whenever she tried to speak, she could only make that sound. Pepin ordered a committee to visit Varennes and ascertain the truth of the situation, which they confirmed.

Gangolf is invoked for household peace and, peculiarly, the healing of paronychia, a disease of finger- and toenails. Farmers in France have a saying: "If it rains on the feast of St. Gengoul [Gangolf], then of acorns the pigs will have their fill."[2]

WHY ST. GANGOLF DESERVES OUR ATTENTION AND DEVOTION

As Pope Paul VI predicted, marital infidelity has become common in our age.[3] Once a married person betrays his or her spouse, forgiveness is incredibly hard, and understandably so. Nonetheless, forgiving is crucial. If we don't forgive, our hurt and anger can morph into a cancer that will devour the marrow of our families. Marriages can survive infidelity. They can't survive an unforgiving heart.

Though his forgiveness was unrequited, St. Gangolf shows us through the clemency he offered Ganea how to act in the face of betrayal. Forgiveness is always the better way.

Jesus, you told us to forgive seventy times seven. When someone hurts us, help us hurdle our granite wall of pain and anger to do that. Help us overcome the fear of being hurt again. Help us regain trust by first putting our trust in you. Then, please, gently guide us toward healing and reconciliation. Lord, we know you can do this, for you can do all things.

St. Benoît d'Aniane

So Important Yet So Forgotten

ca. 752–February 11, 821 • Pre-Congregation

Memorial: February 11

What if a famous historical figure whose name you recognized and whose deeds you memorized in school became someone so obscure that twelve hundred years later only scholars would know him? This has happened with St. Benoît d'Aniane. He was arguably the most influential man of his time, yet who remembers him today?

Given the ever-popular boy's name Wittiza at birth, he was educated at the court of King Pepin the Younger (714–768). Wittiza so impressed everyone that His Majesty made him the *échanson* for his wife, Bertha, which meant he had to procure fitting wines for the queen. His standing only increased under Pepin's son, Charlemagne, because of the valor he showed in a 774 campaign against the barbarian Lombards in Italy. His was a rising star.

However, following the Battle of Pavia, he barely saved his brother from drowning in the Ticino River. For three years Wittiza had increasingly come to recognize the emptiness of worldly life, and his brother's near-death experience clinched that perception. As a result he entered a Benedictine abbey, taking the name Benoît (pronounced *Ben-wah*, meaning "Benedict"). He threw himself wholly into his order's way of life, adopted ascetic habits, and devoted himself to learning more about the order's rule.

After just six years at the abbey, Benoît had so impressed his fellows that they unanimously elected him abbot. At the same time, his unending asceticism annoyed them. He didn't care to govern these undisciplined men either. After all, if they had no interest in following his example, why would they respect his leadership?

As Vicar Isaac Smith writes, monastic life at this time was excellent in some places but beyond horrid in others. For instance, Benedictines took a vow of poverty, yet many monasteries had immense wealth. Monks were to elect their abbot, but the king often filled the position, usually with a layman. Although the rule called for cloistered monks, many came and went at will. And since monks often went from one monastery to another with great ease, those with a poor formation "infected" others.[1]

Benoît moved back to his home region to live as a hermit. Two monks subsequently joined him, and together they founded the Abbey of Aniane in 782.

The community grew rapidly, thanks to several factors. First, there were Benoît's tremendous qualities and his insistence on faithfulness to both the gospel and the Benedictine rule. Some of his innovations became hallmarks of monastic life: the faithful praying of the Divine Office, its timetable and substance, the monks' clothing, and much more. He insisted on manual labor, since a community's abandonment of this often led to its abandonment of the rule's other parts. And in an age when priestly formation was often grossly deficient, many diocesan priests discovered that Benoît's monasteries offered the best training for their vocations. Aniane soon became the mold and hub for Western monastic reform. Benoît sent out over three hundred monks either to establish new monasteries or to reform monasteries that had become lax.

Sadly, that was a good proportion of them, and this just dismayed Emperor Charlemagne (742–814). It worsened his already healthy distrust of men who wanted to live outside of the world, even if it was for love of God. Therefore, he insisted that abbots make work and prayer their primary goals, with the greater emphasis on prayer. The reason would amaze us today. His empire was enormous, and he knew how weak he and his administrators were. Thus he believed right governance and the common good demanded the prayers of these cloistered men. The empire needed monastic reform and the emperor recognized that Benoît was the only man for the job.

One mark of Charlemagne's confidence in Benoît was that he sent him to Spain to fight the heresy of adoptionism, which said Jesus was the Son of God by adoption and his baptism from John the Baptist. Charlemagne's confidence was well placed, and the heresy died a quick death.

Charlemagne's son and successor, Louis the Pious (778–840), supported Benoît even more. He wanted Benoît's reforms to be the religious link that united his empire, which included almost all of Western Europe and parts of Eastern Europe. He installed Benoît in an abbey near his capital at Inden, so they could coordinate their efforts. Part of this entailed the emperor's appointing men to conduct "visitations" or investigations of monasteries.

Despite this flagrant alliance between church and state, no one complained of "theocracy." Rather it was a time of peace and prosperity for the common people.

With the emperor's backing, Benoît put a stop to the nobility's theft of monastic revenues, which were often more considerable than their own. He additionally prevented nobles from appointing puppet abbots in their fiefdoms and pleaded with the emperor against the nobles when they oppressed people. Such actions earned him their enmity. His no-nonsense style had the same effect on many monks.

Benoît didn't care. God had given him this task, and he would do it regardless. Interestingly, several nobles moved from disliking him to entering his monastery. What impressed so many was the man's utter lack of hypocrisy. He practiced all he preached.

Benoît's impact on our world wasn't limited to monastic reform. Aiding Charlemagne's efforts to increase literacy, he promoted the use of lowercase script, which enabled writing from one part of the empire to be legible in every other part. He also increased the number of books available in monastic scriptoria. And so he played a key role in the development of culture, the fruits of which we still enjoy today.

Benoît never stopped working for reform. Sadly, many monasteries did not accept his guidance. And after his death in 821, his work collapsed in almost every monastery, except those he had personally founded or reformed. It took another two hundred years before his vision became self-sustaining.

WHY ST. BENOÎT DESERVES OUR ATTENTION AND DEVOTION

St. Benoît had a tremendous impact on our culture. More to the point, however, he teaches an important lesson: Since its earliest days, the authority of the Church (see Acts 15:1–21), which Christ himself ordained (see Matthew 16:16–20; 18:18; John 20:21), has given us a sure framework by which to apprehend the gentle persuasions of the Holy Spirit. Benoît recognized this, and his insistence on it has served the Church and our world well.

Lord, you know the difficulties leaders face, the resistance to change, the lack of cooperation, the pride that gets in the way of reform. Despite such frustrations, St. Benoît reposed his trust in you and let nothing stop him from accomplishing your will. Through his prayers, help us do the same.

St. Rasso of Andechs
The Gentle Giant
ca. 880–d. 953 • Pre-Congregation
Memorial: May 17 and June 19

Take a history book off the shelf. Open it and start thumbing through the pages. As your fingers turn the leaves, don't just scan. Hunt for the epic turning points, the decisive events such as battles or treaties or technological advances. Notice the individuals mentioned in relation to these events. Some names we don't know, but we have at least heard of others: Napoleon, Julius Caesar, Cleopatra, Joan of Arc, Thomas Edison, and so forth. What is missing from this picture, though? What is missing are those who made it possible for the major players to succeed. Most of them are not even a footnote. We have totally forgotten them.

For instance, consider St. Rasso, a six-foot-six giant whose gentlemanly bearing was as impressive as his stature. His great height and the formidable military skills he honed in many jousting tournaments combined to make him a great warrior. His finest moments in this regard were his valorous and crucial efforts in two decisive battles. These not only cemented his reputation as a top soldier but arguably contributed to changing German history.

The first was the Battle of Welser Heide in 942, and the other the Battle of Mauerkirchen in 948. Both were fought to defend Bavaria from the marauding Magyars, who would eventually establish Hungary. These barbarians regularly raided rural villages and looted cities, taking with them not only booty but slaves. Both battles were fairly decisive defeats for the Magyars, bringing peace to the Bavarian people for many years.

Not long after the last battle, Rasso laid aside his arms and accompanied Duchess Judith, wife of Duke Henry I of Bavaria and daughter of the Holy Roman Emperor Arnulf of Carinthia, on a pilgrimage to both Jerusalem and Rome. When he returned he built the monastery we now call Grafrath (which means "Count Rasso") and bestowed on it relics he had collected in the Holy Land. Then, having settled his affairs, he became a monk. He lived the last two years of his life at Grafrath in humble servitude. His acts of spiritual generosity reportedly put his battlefield accomplishments to shame.

After his death it was not the relics from the Holy Land but his own that drew the most pilgrims. Between 1444 and 1728, over 12,130 miracles occurred through prayers at his tomb. There were many healings from stomach illness and kidney stones and many healings of children.

Why St. Rasso deserves our attention and devotion

Many so badly want to leave a mark on the world before they die. Programs such as *Britain's Got Talent* or *American Idol*, not to mention professional sports and so many other endeavors, wouldn't exist if people didn't crave everlasting fame and the material wealth that often accompanies it. Nor is that anything new. The lust for celebrity has driven men since at least the time of Homer. Had St. Rasso merely sought his fame as the great warrior he was, he would be less than a footnote today in that history book we thumbed through at the beginning of the chapter: We would have utterly forgotten him. Instead, we remember him for the sanctity that made his heavenly intercession before God so effective.

It's not that earthly accomplishments aren't important. Rather, we need to ensure that they're not motivated by mere earthly ambition but by zeal for the honor and glory of God.

Lord, let me never fall into the trap of pride, which turns people away from you and toward their own quasi-deification. Through St. Rasso's example and prayers, please help me avoid that quicksand. And if I fall, please rescue me right away. Through your powerful name, Lord Jesus, and the intercession of your most Blessed Virgin Mother.

St. Hemma of Gurk
Widening the Eye of the Needle
ca. 980–June 17, 1045 • Canonized: January 5, 1938
Memorial: June 27

When Jesus said, "You [will] always have the poor with you" (Matthew 26:11), he wasn't saying we could ignore them. In fact, throughout the Gospels, our Lord makes it clear that we must care for the needy (see Matthew 25:31–46, for example).

However, when we reach a certain level of affluence—whether personally or societally—it is so easy to ignore the poor, isn't it? Our neighborhoods are removed from theirs. Our struggles can be different. Still, we can't use what separates us as an excuse to keep us apart. We must do something, but what? Like our next saint, we can grow in the heroic generosity that holds nothing back and is key to understanding our Lord's command to "love your neighbor as yourself" (Matthew 22:39).

The only certain thing we know about St. Hemma of Gurk's early life is that she came from Austria's ranking nobility and was somehow related to Holy Roman Emperor St. Henry II. As was customary, Henry's wife, Empress St. Cunigunde, reared Hemma at court. She could not have had a better teacher. To understand why, you must first understand Her Majesty.

First, Cunigunde was agonizingly awkward around other people. She wanted to be liked and have friends, so this deeply pained her. She had so many around her, but she was all alone.

Furthermore, while she often experienced long periods of God's presence in prayer, at other times Our Savior let her experience what mystics call the Dark Night. That is when it seems God is nowhere to be found, and it is often accompanied by great suffering. Knowing our good Savior would never allow these burdensome experiences were it not somehow for her good (see Jeremiah 29:11–14), Cunigunde learned to turn them into a form of prayer. In turn, this radical reliance on God profoundly deepened her faith and trust in him.

As a result, Cunigunde didn't just train Hemma in the earthly skills necessary to her state in life. She also taught her the vastly more important spiritual habits she would need. After all, history is studded with persons who allowed privilege and power to lead them away from God. The empress even taught her how to invest all of her earthly duties with a sense of prayer and piety.

Finally, if ever there arose in Cunigunde's schooling of Hemma a conflict between teaching the material or the spiritual, the spiritual unfailingly won out. Today's equivalent might be, "I don't care if the championship soccer game takes place on Sunday at 10 AM and your team needs you to win. That's the only time we can go to Mass this weekend, and this family doesn't miss Mass. Ever. For any reason unless you're too sick to get out of bed. Or an emergency. The Third Commandment does not have an escape clause that says "…unless you have an important soccer game to play." On coming of age, Hemma married Count Wilhelm von Friesach, who was landed, wealthy, and powerful.

Like the Bible's Hannah, Hemma had difficulty conceiving. After ten years of trying, the countess clothed herself in the meager, practically threadbare attire of a pilgrim and proceeded to walk barefoot to three Marian pilgrimage sites in southern Austria. She would pray that through the intercession of his own Blessed Mother, God the Son would hear her prayers to become a mother, too.

After she had visited the first two, she began making her way toward the third. She felt so miserable, however, that even her desperate desire to bear children almost didn't keep her going forward. You see, the journey had been a bone-chilling, rain-drenched, and muddy one. Owing to this, Hemma caught some illness or other, and it completely sapped her strength.

As you can imagine, she reached that last site exhausted and feeling like she wanted to die. Her ordeal wasn't over, however. Looking up, she saw that the third shrine sat atop a steep hill. She felt crushed and began sobbing and collapsed in a heap on the waterlogged, miry ground. In a short while, though, she told herself she had come this far, and she would not let this last obstacle stop her when none of the others had. So with great effort, like Our Lord after his third fall on the way to Calvary, she climbed it and, entering the shrine, embraced its statue of the Virgin. Then Hemma fainted on the spot and slept undisturbed for three days. Not long thereafter, she delivered two sons.

By 1036, Hemma's husband and children had died. Given the resources she had brought into the marriage and those she had received from her husband, she ranked among the world's wealthiest women. Besides land, she owned markets and tariff routes, and Henry II had given her coinage rights.

Cunigunde had piously raised Hemma to serve the Lord by serving others, so she used her wealth to establish several foundations and houses to aid the poor. The rough conditions of peasant life back then make the fact that so many survived a testament to human hardiness. Without Hemma's assistance, though, many more would not have withstood the harsh winters and scarcity of food. Maybe some readers of this book exist only because she fed and sheltered their ancestors.

Hemma also used her wealth to construct at least ten additional churches in an area that had just twenty. In this way she greatly increased the local population's access to the sacraments, which likely kept the faith alive in certain families (maybe those of your ancestors?).

One legend associated with Hemma is that of the fair wage. During the construction of Gurk's cathedral, which she funded and oversaw, the workers demanded higher wages. On payday, Hemma insisted on paying the laborers herself. She invited each to take from the payroll purse what he thought he deserved. No matter how greedily someone grabbed inside, his hand drew out the same sum he had already been receiving. St. Hemma died a poor religious in a convent she had helped found. Since 1228 authorities have catalogued over one hundred sixty miracles for people praying at her sepulcher, including the raising of two children from the dead. Until myriad political situations in the twentieth century caused the cessation of pilgrimages to her tomb, they attracted hundreds each year. Thankfully, pilgrimages have started to pick back up again.

WHY ST. HEMMA DESERVES OUR ATTENTION AND DEVOTION

St. Hemma shows, among many other things, that being rich is not in and of itself a sin. While our Lord said it was harder for the rich to enter heaven than for a camel to pass through a needle's eye, he added that "with God all things are possible" (Matthew 19:24).

The sin comes when we think our wealth is ours. Instead we're called to be God's charity arm, to show heroic generosity. For "every one to whom much is given, of him will much be required" (Luke 12:48).

Lord, thank you for your poor. They serve as constant reminders of our debt to you for your generosity and for any good we possess. St. Hemma recognized this and served them with the blessings you gave her. Teach us to do the same. Help us lighten their load, regardless of the cost.

Bl. Gezelinus
The Least Significant Saint Ever?
ca. 1070–August 6, 1149 • Pre-Congregation

Memorial: August 6

Few saints merit the title "holy unknown" as much as St. Gezelinus. That, however, is not the main reason you are reading his story. Rather, it is because he shows how anyone can become a saint. We don't need to preach great sermons or leap tall buildings in a single bound. All we have to do is know, love, and serve Our Lord with all our body and soul. Granted, that's hard to consistently do. For a long time, though, it wasn't easy for him, either. So he also shows how things get easier the more we do them.

Born in the early twelfth century and named after a seventh-century saint, Gezelinus entered the monastery at Morimond, France, in an effort to renounce the world. When the abbot decided to establish another foundation at Altenberg in 1132, he sent Gezelinus there and gave him responsibility for tending the sheep. This often meant he had to move the herd to large pastures, where he was the only monk around. He came to like this solitude, and he lived this way for fourteen years in the mountains and valleys nearby. The remoteness allowed him to pray and open his heart to God, and because of this, he became perfectly content and happy.

Gezelinus's expertise in animal husbandry made him invaluable to the locals. His holiness also endeared him to them, and they came to see him as their spiritual leader.

Once the region suffered a tremendous drought that dried up all its streams and wells. The people pleaded with Gezelinus to beseech God for water. Like a modern-day Moses, Gezelinus bowed his head in prayer and struck the ground with his shepherd's staff. Water flowed. It still flows today, enclosed in a special chapel called the Gezelinquelle. The water is thought to be especially good against eye problems, childhood diseases, bad headaches, and animal diseases.

Gezelinus died in 1149. Over the centuries the location of his tomb was lost to memory, but it was rediscovered in 1810. In 1903, Church authorities transferred his coffin to the parish Church of St. Andrew. At one time huge pilgrimages marked his feast day. Like St. Patrick's Day celebrations in some places, however, these events came to resemble raucous parties more than a festive commemoration of a saint. This and other factors caused the flow of pilgrims to shrivel over time. Pilgrimages to the shrine have resumed but are much fewer than before.

WHY BL. GEZELINUS DESERVES OUR ATTENTION AND DEVOTION

When next you drive past a cemetery, think of how many saints might be there who, like St. Gezelinus, never did big things. They simply loved the Lord with all their mind, heart, and soul. The wonderful thing is that this way is open to all of us. It's not easy—no path to sanctity ever is—but it is doable with prayer, frequent recourse to the sacraments, constant effort, and God's grace.

Holy Spirit, we praise you for the witness of Bl. Gezelinus's life, which flowed with the life-giving water promised by Our Lord. In Jesus' name, help us follow his example.

St. Elin of Skövde

You Can't Keep a Good Well Down

ca. 1101–August 1, 1160 • Canonized: 1165

Memorial: July 30 or 31

When someone falsely accuses us or accuses us of having bad will, it can give us a helpless, bewildered, even crestfallen feeling. How, though, as Christians do we deal with those moments? Our next saint shows us one possible way.

St. Elin of Skövde was a wealthy married woman with many children. Her husband died young, leaving her to raise her family and manage their farm. Despite such a hectic, never-a-dull-moment life, she still found time to aid the local poor. She gave generously to her parish, which was built largely with her wealth and oversight. Legend says that she insisted on keeping a space between the vestibule and the bell tower of the church, with the hope that God would provide a saint's relics to place there. He did: hers.

At some point Elin decided to go on pilgrimage to the Holy Land. This trip, though it would help her grow closer to God, would also be her downfall.

One of Elin's daughters had married a powerful and abusive man. He was cruel not only toward his wife but also toward his workers, who absolutely hated him. One day they decided they'd had enough and killed the bully. When this man's relatives found the culprits and were about to kill them there and then, the murderers falsely claimed Elin had put them up to it. They noted her Holy Land pilgrimage began right after her son-in-law's murder. Perhaps she hoped to give herself an alibi. What if the trip was her required penance for so awful a crime? The man's relatives convinced themselves that she was guilty.

After her return, Elin learned of the accusation. Furthermore, the relatives began threatening her. When she protested her innocence, it just made them more convinced. She began praying for them, instead. Notice, she didn't pray for her protection. She prayed for them.

One day, she travelled from Skövde to Götene to attend the consecration of that village's new church, since she had helped fund it. It was during her walk there that the kin of Elin's son-in-law ambushed and killed her. So violent was their assault, they severed clean a finger bearing a ring she'd purchased in the Holy Land.

God wrought miracles through Elin's intercession almost immediately. At dusk a young boy was leading a blind man down the road to Götene when he saw a light in the bushes. A closer investigation revealed the severed finger. The child handed it to his sightless companion. Some of the still-fresh blood got on his finger, and the blind man inadvertently rubbed his eye with the blood. God restored his sight.

Pope Alexander III canonized St. Elin around 1165. Although she died on August 1, that feast date was already occupied, so her feast is celebrated July 30 or 31, depending on the locale.

Skövde kept her relics in its renamed St. Elin Church, and her sepulcher became a primary Scandinavian pilgrimage site. Indeed, her shrine made the former backwater a thriving city. During the Protestant revolt, Lutherans buried her relics in a secret place. Even so, as late as the mid–nineteenth century, pilgrims came to her former burial place to collect little bags of earth. They left crutches and votive offerings in gratitude for favors received.

In 1596 the Lutherans took refuse and stopped up a brook a little ways outside of Skövde called St. Elin's Spring. Legend says that this stream had burst forth when Elin's body was carried into town for her funeral. Its waters were supposedly miraculous. The well burst forth again recently, and pilgrims have begun to return.

WHY ST. ELIN DESERVES OUR ATTENTION AND DEVOTION
It's painful when someone falsely accuses us of wrongdoing or even of doing something completely neutral (e.g., being loud) but doing so out of ill will ("You're doing that on purpose to bother me!"), as if they can know the disposition of our hearts. St. Elin faced this situation and confidently placed herself in God's hands. Yes, she lost her life, but look at her heavenly reward. Trust God.

God our Father, help your children to always assume goodwill and to approach each other with the utmost charity.

St. Drogo of Sebourg
The Ugly Nobleman Shepherd
1118–April 16, ca. 1185 • Pre-Congregation
Memorial: April 16

God didn't create us for suffering, but because of the Fall, suffering affects all of us. Furthermore, God often allows suffering, since it helps us discern the true, the good, and the beautiful and to distinguish it from the appalling counterfeits offered by a lonely, desperate, grasping world.

Consider, for instance, St. Drogo. Born of noble blood, he lost both his parents early on, his mother while giving birth to him. As a child, he must have often thought about his mother and felt her absence and longed for her presence terribly, for every child needs its mother. Therefore, when during his teen years he learned the circumstances of her death, he was so wracked by guilt that he began doing extreme penances.

On reaching adulthood, Drogo gave the poor his wealth and walked to Sebourg, France. There he spent the next six years as a shepherd for the noblewoman Elizabeth de la Haire. Think of it: A person raised in comfort becomes a shepherd, wears threadbare clothes, and eats very little in order to expiate through prayer and penance an unnecessary guilt. Also, consider that unlike other saints who willingly went from rich to poor, Drogo did not do this because he thought it was God's will for him. Rather, he did it to atone for a tragedy that wasn't his fault. How much, how painfully did he have to torture himself to take such a step? But God used Drogo's pain to take him from a world filled with material cravings and their accompanying spiritual dangers and into one where his greatest desire was closeness to God.

At first Drogo found the shepherd's life very difficult. Slowly, however, his situation came to give him great joy. Indeed, everyone who came in contact with him immediately recognized not only his happiness but also his humility, patience, and kindness. They admired his recollection in prayer. They were awed by his simple spiritual advice. They watched in quiet wonder as he gave to the poor the beautiful presents others had given him.

Eventually Drogo became a sheep expert, and his knowledge of these animals was sought far and wide. At a time when veterinary medicine was still in its infancy, he taught others ways to protect their flocks from disease and provide them with better nutrition. This accounts in part for the past popularity of his patronage among Europe's peasant farmers.

Somehow Drogo developed a hideous facial deformity that made little children cry. Then came ulcers that gave him a stench no one could stomach, even from several yards away. Because of this, he spent his last forty years as an anchorite, a hermit living in a hut built against the side of a church. For sustenance, he ate only barley mixed with ashes and water and the Eucharist.

That anyone would purposefully choose a dish that features ashes as an ingredient is hard to fathom, but no more so than a woman choosing to endure labor or a man choosing to dash into a burning house to save his family. After all, love enables us to do tremendous things and makes possible otherwise inconceivable sacrifices. Indeed, love involves sacrifice by definition.

God must have loved Drogo right back. A fire once reduced his cell to ashes. During the conflagration Drogo never budged, yet he suffered not even a slight burn.

WHY ST. DROGO DESERVES OUR ATTENTION AND DEVOTION

Suffering is not good, but it can produce good. God sometimes uses it to awaken us and to draw us closer to him by showing both his strength and our absolute reliance on that strength. Christ took St. Drogo's tears of sadness and shame and turned them into tears of peace and joy. He can do the same for you.

Loving God, you allowed St. Drogo's heartbreak to reveal a glimpse of your magnificence. Through his prayers and example, enable us to use our suffering to grow in holiness and show forth your amazing glory.

St. Homobonus Tucenghi of Cremona
Henpecked for Holiness
ca. 1117–November 13, 1197 • Canonized: 1199
Memorial: November 13

Since our Lord told us that "the world will hate you because of me" (see John 15:18–19), we expect harassment from those who hate Christ. But what if we receive such treatment from someone who is both a fellow Christian and sacramentally pledged to love us? And what if this behavior is done to pressure us into no longer serving Jesus? Like our current saint, we choose Christ.

Because his middle-class parents wanted to give their son a name he would have to live up to, they chose Homobonus, which means, literally, "good man." When his father passed away, Homobonus inherited the family's wool business, and it steadily grew under his management, and did so simply because he was honest.

Even though he was honest, however, that doesn't mean he was always a saint. For a long time Homobonus was just a normal businessman trying to grow his company and reap the fruits of his successful labors. Around age fifty, he had to handle an exceptionally large amount of money. Suddenly his hands turned black and, no matter how he washed them, they wouldn't come clean. Deeply alarmed, he frantically sought out a holy priest and asked him to explain what was happening. All the cleric told him was, "Go, sell what you possess and give the proceeds to the poor" (see Luke 18:22).

So while he may not have started out particularly concerned about sanctity, from that point on Homobonus worked hard to grow in piety and heroic generosity to the underprivileged. His own house was the epicenter of his activities. The poor slept there, ate there, and received alms, jobs, and medical treatment there. Furthermore, often it was Homobonus who cared for them. When they died, he personally helped with their burial.

You see, Homobonus believed God had given him a good inheritance and made him successful so he could be Christ to the impoverished. Thus, money was simply a means for him, not an end. The poor clearly had rights to it. As the Church has always taught, we must not hoard our material blessings. Rather we should use them to relieve others' poverty. Homobonus's actions, therefore, anticipated saints such as Francis de Sales and Josemaría Escrivá, who taught us to work out our salvation in the duties of our particular state (see Philippians 2:12).

The Tucenghi family lived comfortably but simply so there would be more money for Homobonus's apostolate. So generous was he, in fact, that in Cremona, when someone made an excessive request for money, the response would be, "I don't have the purse of St. Homobonus!"

Sadly, this did not sit well with his wife. Her husband had the means to indulge her with luxury; instead she ate and dressed simply. This greatly interfered with the lifestyle to which she wanted to grow accustomed. As a result, she constantly nagged Homobonus to use more of their wealth for their family. In this way she became his cross rather than his helpmate. He simply prayed for her conversion and continued his work.

Homobonus's charity earned him immense respect, which made him highly influential. While other Italian city-states were wracked with violence because of the medieval tensions between the Guelphs and Ghibellines (that is, between those who supported papal authority and those who supported imperial authority), in Cremona, Homobonus got everyone to disagree without being disagreeable. It was one of medieval Italy's most livable places.

Of course, social justice without prayer is simply social work in nicer dress. Homobonus didn't let that happen. Rather, in him were married an intense spiritual devotion and a total self-donation to the poor, each constantly feeding into the other. Daily Mass was an important part of his spiritual regimen. So it was that during Mass one morning, the congregation was praying the Gloria when Homobonus stretched out his arms and fell forward. (Back then churches did not have pews.) He had done the same thing before. The people around him probably figured, "Oh, that Homobonus. There he goes, being penitential again." They discovered he had died only when he didn't stand up for the Gospel.

Owing to the scads of eye-popping miracles at his tomb, Pope Innocent III canonized Homobonus a mere fourteen months after his passing, with the bull *Quia Pietas*. This made Homobonus the first lay saint who was not a noble to be formally canonized.

WHY ST. HOMOBONUS DESERVES OUR ATTENTION AND DEVOTION

In *Quia Pietas*, Innocent wrote, "Two things are required for someone to be reputed a saint: virtue of morals and the truth of signs, which is to say, works of piety in life and the manifestation of miracles after death."[1] Homobonus had both. He knew that his material success was not his own doing, and its fruits were not solely for himself or his family. He lived as if he knew from memory the proverb that says, "The dark side of an answered prayer is that we end up forgetting Him Who has helped us.

Holy God, you inspired St. Homobonus to understand that what you give is not to be kept and hoarded but to be shared for building the kingdom of heaven. By his ardent prayers, help us know what things we can do, small or great, to relieve others' misery to the degree our station in life allows. We ask this in your holy name.

St. Pietro Parenzo

There's a Politician in Heaven

d. May 21, 1199 • Canonized: 1879

Memorial: May 21

An hour north of Rome, beyond the dreamily bucolic countryside of Lazio and Umbria, stands the fairy-tale town of Orvieto. One moment all that lies before the traveler is plain. The next moment a huge rock crowned by a once-impregnable fortress juts out of the ground, and it is immediately apparent why popes sought safety here in times of danger.

During the Middle Ages popes were not the only visitors. Pilgrims by the millions made their way to this welcoming city on a hill. Sure, Orvieto was a good place to rest before pushing on to Rome, but it also provided its own attraction: the tomb of a saint from whom miracles by the dozens were obtained.

Who was this man who provided a reason for droves of pilgrims to trudge up the steep incline from the plain to the city's duomo (cathedral)? St. Pietro Parenzo. Heard of him? Don't feel bad; few have. But his story is a great one.

At the time our saint lived, Orvieto was in the throes of the most enduring struggle of medieval Italy, that between the Guelphs and the Ghibellines. Essentially, the Guelphs were loyal to the pope and supported papal power, while the Ghibellines supported the Holy Roman Emperor. It was not unusual for passing bands of Guelphs and Ghibellines to get into knife fights, which then prompted desires for *vendette*, creating a spiraling cycle of violence. Two successive bishops, Rustico and Ricardo, had actually encouraged this situation over several decades.

The Cathar heresy was also going full-steam in many places, including Orvieto. Its adherents believed there were two gods: The first, Rex Mundi, created the world, which was evil and chaotic. It stood to reason, therefore, that everything material was evil. The other god created all that was spiritual and therefore good.

The Cathari believed that their purpose in life was to transcend the material in order to achieve the purely spiritual. Thus marriage and procreation were evil, since they helped perpetuate the material. Suicide, on the other hand, was good because it helped people transcend the material.

Cathari also denied Jesus' divinity. They preached that the beauty so valued by the Church was proof of its being under the sway of Rex Mundi. The Cathari in Orvieto were largely Ghibellines, whose religious convictions simply provided another way for them to express their antipapal political beliefs. This heresy was powerful and hugely popular in many places, including Orvieto.

For these reasons Pope Innocent III had placed the town under interdict in 1198. Into this chaos he sent Pietro Parenzo, a married layman, to serve as mayor. His Holiness gave Pietro two goals: strengthen the faith by fighting heresy and make peace between the different parties. Mayor Parenzo decided that the best strategy was to get tough with troublemakers, so the first thing he did upon taking office was to abolish the traditional carnival games, on the grounds that these sports were often used as a ruse to commit homicide.

Such law-and-order efforts cheered the town's Catholics but incensed the Cathari. To spite the mayor and to flex their muscles, they came to the Carnival festivities brandishing swords and other weapons, and they started fights with people at random. Riots ensued.

Into this melee of flying sharp steel rode Pietro without receiving a scratch. Identifying the culprits, he authorized the destruction of their families' towers—symbols of power in medieval Italy—and their palaces. The common people cheered Mayor Parenzo. It was about time someone did something about those troublemaking ruffians, by gummit. The heretics, on the other hand, seethed.

In all his efforts Pietro worked closely with the repentant Bishop Ricardo, even living in His Excellency's palace. The good of the Church was seen as the good of the state and vice versa, so this arrangement was not remarkable. Together they announced an amnesty program: Return to the Church by a certain date, and all would be forgiven. Ignore the deadline, however, and face stiff fines.

Pietro also exacted a form of bail to ensure good behavior on the part of some citizens. While the amounts were fair and did deter crime, he now had even more enemies, and these began to plot his death.

At Easter Pietro returned to Rome to brief His Holiness on his efforts. He also confided to him that his life was in danger. Innocent lauded his good work and encouraged him to continue with caution, but he also made a point of hearing the young man's confession. Before saying good-bye to his wife and mother, Pietro made out his will.

A huge crowd greeted his return to Orvieto on May 1, 1199. He told the people that if he were to die, it would be to defend the holy Catholic faith. On May 21, 1199, nearly three weeks later, a traitorous servant named Radulfo let the heretics into the bishop's palace. They captured Pietro as he undressed for bed, beat him, and smuggled him out of the city to a safe house in the countryside.

His captors offered him a deal: Repeal the rules restricting their efforts, repay the fines and sureties he had exacted, resign his position, and give their religious beliefs preferential treatment. Pietro agreed to return the fines out of his own funds, but he had pledged to defend the faith and so refused to support them in their heresy. Enraged, one of his captors bashed his head with a hammer. The sight and smell of freshly spilled blood excited his captors, who fell on him in a demonic frenzy. Those who couldn't land blows tore hair from his head. Then they dumped his corpse by a tree and fled.

Six monks found Pietro's body at dawn the next day. The whole city poured down the hill, weeping piteously at the gruesome sight. The bishop and other clergy accompanied his remains back into the city with great pomp and buried him in the duomo. His death prompted a great reaction against the Cathari. Nonetheless, it was not until the late 1260s that the heresy was eradicated.

Soon the people were venerating Pietro as a martyr. During the Middle Ages his tomb attracted pilgrims by the millions. While his cause never went through the formal canonization process, Leo XIII approved his cult in 1879.

Today, however, most tourists bypass Orvieto. The main draw for those who visit the cathedral is a eucharistic miracle; the saint's tomb is easily missed. St. Pietro has been largely forgotten.

WHY ST. PIETRO PARENZO DESERVES OUR
ATTENTION AND DEVOTION

Defying popular opinion, doing the right thing, and standing with the Church are not easy. Never have been, never will be. Thus, in many respects, the challenges that confronted St. Pietro are the same ones we encounter in our age.

Help us to see, Lord, how you would have us imitate St. Pietro's constancy and fidelity to you and your holy Church. Give us courage, strength, patience, and above all the ability to love with your love.

St. Bona of Pisa

Come Fly With Me, Let's Fly, Let's Fly Away

ca. 1156–May 29, 1207 • Non causa

Memorial: May 29

An advertisement that plays on American Catholic radio stations has a great tagline: "If you're baptized, you're a missionary." Hearing this is arresting, because most Catholics don't consider themselves missionaries. And yet the Gospels make clear our duty to evangelize. Just how is that done? As St. Bona shows, however you can.

When Bona was three years old, her father, Bernardo, left the family with nothing but crushing debt. Rather than allow Bona to wallow in sadness, her mother instructed her to pray and to cast all her sorrows, cares, and aspirations on God. So the little girl spent long hours in Pisa's Holy Sepulcher Church.

This is where, at age seven, Bona had her first vision, when the crucifix reached out to her. Another really frightening vision featured our Lord, the Blessed Virgin Mary, and three saints, including the apostle James the Greater. The small girl fled from the church, but James followed and lovingly calmed her. He then kindly brought her back into church, and from this experience she developed a lifelong devotion to him.

At age fourteen, Bona went alone on pilgrimage to the Holy Land, where Our Lord had revealed that Bernardo was fighting for King Amalric I of Jerusalem in his unsuccessful invasion of Egypt. Whether it was a happy reunion or one that left her feeling rejected and broken-hearted, we don't know. What we do know is that Muslim pirates captured and imprisoned her on her return voyage. Fortunately, some fellow Pisans rescued her.

Going on pilgrimage can be addictive. Maybe this is why she took a large group on a thousand-mile pilgrimage to the shrine of St. James the Greater at Compostela, Spain, a short time after her return. She proved good at leading people on this journey and went on to lead so many pilgrimages there—nine—that she was made an official guide. One report says that Bona was "full of energy, helpful, and unselfish, ready to reassure with her smile those who were sick."[1] Many souls grew closer to Christ through her kindness.

On her tenth trip to Compostela, Bona herself fell sick. On returning home she died.

Bona is the patron not only of pilgrims and guides but also of flight attendants, made so by Pope John XXIII.

WHY ST. BONA DESERVES OUR ATTENTION AND DEVOTION

St. Bona teaches that evangelizing doesn't require theological degrees or great communication abilities or charisma or anything other than what God has given you. As the Second Vatican Council's *Dogmatic Constitution on the Church* puts it: "The lay apostolate [that is, the efforts of the laity on behalf of Christ and his Church]…is a participation in the salvific mission of the Church itself…. The laity are called in a special way to make the Church present and operative in those places and circumstances where only through them can it become the salt of the earth. Thus every layman, in virtue of the very gifts bestowed upon him, is…a witness and a living instrument of the mission of the Church itself 'according to the measure of Christ's bestowal'" (*Lumen Gentium*, 33). Therefore, can you teach, sing, tend, serve? What you can do, do that for his greater glory.

Holy Spirit, after we tend to the need for our own humility and heart's conversion, let us assist you in the work of loving and converting souls to your holy Church. We ask this in Jesus' holy name, through the prayers of St. Bona and of the Blessed Virgin Mary.

Bl. Jacoba de' Settesoli

St. Francis' Other "Beloved Lady"

ca. 1192–February 8, 1239 • Non cultus

Memorial: February 8

A basic catechetical question is "Why did God make you?" and the answer is: "He made me to know him, to love him, and to serve him in this life, so that I may be happy with him forever in heaven." But just how do we do this? By knowing, loving, and serving others.

Now, it's true: God singularly made women and men as helpmates to each other in matrimony (see Genesis 2:18–25). However, matrimony is a reflection of the love we find within the Holy Trinity, a love that holds nothing back. God calls us to make all our relationships like that (see Deuteronomy 6:5; Matthew 25:31–46; Mark 12:30–33).

Few better examples of this exist than Bl. Jacoba de' Settesoli. Born at Torre Astura, she was married to nobleman Graziano Frangipane by at least 1210, and the couple had two sons. Around 1212, she became an early follower of St. Francis after hearing him preach in Rome.

Jacoba asked Francis how she could better practice charity. He replied that as a mother of two and a wife, she should build her holiness in the loving, self-sacrificial practice of her daily duties. In other words, charity begins at home. To help her with this, he guided her toward the Franciscan third order. Indeed, it is because of her that St. Francis may have founded the Franciscan Third Order.

On Graziano's death around 1217, Jacoba became a wealthy woman, owning some of the best real estate in Rome and the surrounding countryside. One of these properties was in Marino, where the locals make *mustaccioli*, a delicious cream-and-honey-filled pastry. Jacoba topped hers with slivered almonds.

Francis and Jacoba became fast friends. In fact, the two were so close that he got away with calling her "Brother Jacoba" because of her somewhat masculine qualities and vigor. He stayed with her when he was in Rome. She doted on him as would a mother, always serving him his fill of *mustaccioli*, which he loved. She also helped the Franciscans purchase land for their first church in Rome.

In recompense for all she did, Francis had Br. James give her a lamb, which followed her everywhere. She wove St. Francis a tunic with its wool.

As his end drew near, Francis decided to write to Jacoba and ask her to bring the necessary materials for his burial. Through the Holy Spirit, however, Jacoba already knew he would soon die. God in turn told Francis, "Stop writing. She already knows."

Jacoba hurried to see him one last time, bringing with her the beloved *mustaccioli* (although he gave them to another, more rotund friar who loved them as much as he), and she stayed at Francis' side for his last four days on earth. After his death she prepared his body for burial, as Mary had done for Jesus, since she considered herself a mother to him. She then wrapped his body in a woolen shroud of her own provision and also helped plan the funeral.

Following his burial, Jacoba settled her affairs in Rome and returned to Assisi, where she spent the rest of her days praying at her best friend's tomb. When she died, the friars positioned her sepulcher to face St. Francis'.

WHY BL. JACOBA DESERVES OUR ATTENTION AND DEVOTION

Bl. Jacoba gives us an excellent example of several things. First, she shows how to become holy within one's vocation. As a widow she exemplifies perseverance in the face of tragedy. Most important, however, is that she demonstrates it's possible to love someone with a totally self-giving love, a love that holds nothing back, that has not a tinge of selfishness. This is the love to which we all are called. "If we love one another, God abides in us and his love is perfected in us" (1 John 4:12).

Lord, you told us to love one another as you loved us. Your faithful love holds nothing back, and it has been fruitful, as evidenced by Christians such as Bl. Jacoba and St. Francis. Help us to have this same self-giving love with everyone in our life, and let this love cover our multitude of sins (see 1 Peter 4:8).

Bl. Piero Tecelano
The Silent Prophet
1190–1289 • Cultus approved: January 2, 1802
Memorial: December 4

Even in the best economies, taxes, regulations, and red tape can make the survival of a small business difficult. Proprietors often lose sleep as they wonder how they'll make payroll or whether they must lay off valued employees. Sometimes they wonder whether they can even keep the doors open. The temptation to cut corners or act unscrupulously must be great. *Il Pettinaio* (the comb maker) helps us see that, in business as in life, honesty is the best policy.

Born outside of Florence to a middle-class family, Piero Tecelano moved to Siena as a child. In time he adopted his father's profession, making and selling combs for hair and looms. Piero grew the company and eventually was able to buy a country house with a vineyard.

At some point Piero realized that money isn't everything. He had a conversion. Prior to this, he had exclusively focused his efforts on satisfying his wants and needs. Now he focused on loving God through generously loving others, even competitors. He and eight merchant and lawyer friends formed a small foundation dedicated to charitable works. Besides giving money, they gave of themselves.

For instance, they personally cleaned the bedpans of the sick and changed their bandages. They visited prisons where conditions were foul. Prisoners at this time received little charity, since most people believed they were only getting what they deserved.

What may have marked Piero most, though, was his honesty. Each month he traveled seventy miles to Pisa and bought combs by the dozens. Before returning home, he would stop on a bridge to inspect his purchases. He threw any defective ones into the Arno River. Someone saw him doing this once and asked him why he didn't sell those imperfect combs at a loss. At least he'd get something for them. Piero replied that he wouldn't want anyone injured while working a loom with one of the defective combs.

Such honesty made Piero Siena's preferred comb merchant, which put his competitors at a considerable disadvantage. Therefore he would purposefully arrive late on market day so his competitors would have a fair shot at selling their wares.

Piero attended daily Mass. Never content with being a mere spectator, he fervently prayed throughout the liturgy. His commitment to the Divine Office was such that the Dominicans extended him the rare privilege of praying it with them. In short, he is probably one of the few in history who could say he successfully followed St. Paul's exhortation to pray ceaselessly (see 1 Thessalonians 5:17).

The Lord did miracles through Piero. For instance, at Mass one day a woman died, and through Piero's prayers God raised her from the dead.

It's easy to understand therefore why people considered Piero a living saint. Some, however, see saints as easy targets. Hoping to trap him, some teens asked what would happen if he found himself in a locked room with a willing, beautiful woman, and no one would ever know what had taken place. He knew what he *should* do, he replied, but until that moment, he did not know what he *would* do. Furthermore, he'd lived his whole life trying to avoid sin, and that's why he always acted as if the whole world was watching. Stunned by such candor, the boys left.

Another time some punks surrounded Piero, threatening him and calling him a sorcerer. He responded in a calm, gentle way and won them over. They marveled aloud that he really was a saint. No one so humble wants to hear himself described in that way, and so he ran off.

Unlike many lay saints of the time, Piero was married and had up to four children. A good and dutiful husband, he always came straight home after work. After his wife died, he sold the house and vineyard and gave the proceeds to the poor. He then became a lay Franciscan and served as an orderly in a Franciscan hospital.

We have no writings by Piero, which is apt for a silent man like him. This explains why pictures depict him with a finger to his lips. The words he did speak, however, carried impressive weight.

For instance, once a con man drained the city's coffers. After speaking with Piero, he returned the money. When the Franciscans couldn't decide whether a prospective novice was a good fit, they had Piero interview him. When Bl. Ambrose Sansedoni balked at becoming a bishop, it was Piero's counsel that persuaded him to take the position.

His taciturnity, however, often frustrated people. For instance, a mayor from a distant city learned of his wise counsel and came to ask his advice. After explaining his problem in detail, the mayor asked Piero what he should do. Piero essentially responded, "Don't offend God."

Piero died surrounded by friends and family, not to mention the local clergy chanting the office for the dying. Being something of a prophet, his last words predicted the downfall of Pistoia, Florence, and his own Siena. Pope Pius VII beatified him in 1802, because of both the endurance of his followers and the many miracles that occurred at his tomb.

WHY BL. PIERO DESERVES OUR ATTENTION AND DEVOTION

Bl. Piero shows two things. The first is that honesty and choosing one's words wisely are indeed the best policies. The second is, be countercultural. The world's focus is on acquiring; if we have disposable income, we think we should save it or spend it. This isn't Christ's focus, though (see Luke 12:13–21; Matthew 25:31–46). Being wealthy is not sinful, as long as we try to be like Piero and remember that we are our brothers' keeper.[1]

Lord, having things feels good. Things are enjoyable, and they give us a sense of security, as though they will protect us from the terrifying state of poverty. Help us remember, though, that we don't keep our checkbooks after death. Through Bl. Piero's prayers, make us generous of heart in order that we might store up treasure in heaven. We ask this in your name.

Bl. Béatrix d'Ornacieux

She Really Nailed Her Love for Jesus

ca. 1260–November 25, 1303 • Cultus approved: April 15, 1869

Memorial: November 25

A man who has plastered his car with hand-painted slogans such as "Abortion is murder!" occasionally attends Mass at our parish. To say the mere presence of the car, garish as it is, makes some people uncomfortable does not do justice to the word *uncomfortable*. They fear he makes believers look like kooks—and really, they worry he makes *them* look bad—although nothing he's written is in any way untrue.

Others take the view that his motorized billboard is obnoxious and does nothing to further the cause. Both groups think the gentleman a fool, but being a fool for Christ isn't a bad thing. St. Paul writes this three times within four chapters of 1 Corinthians (see 1:18; 3:18; 4:10). And if there's an issue with this sincere gentleman making his car a pulpit, what would we think of Bl. Béatrix d'Ornacieux?

Born in southeastern France, Béatrix's father and brother were lords—one brother was a bishop—and she could have had a similar life. Instead, at age thirteen she entered the Parménie Charterhouse. *Charterhouse* signifies a Carthusian convent or monastery. Essentially Carthusians are cenobites, hermits who live in community, and they maintain a vow of silence. This helps them better concentrate on union with God through prayer, which is why Béatrix chose this way of life.

She lived at Parménie for roughly twenty-seven years. Contemporaries noted her ardent love and deep devotion to our Lord's passion. Indeed, her gratitude for Jesus' sacrifice prompted extraordinary efforts to understand and enter into it. During one Lent, for instance, her love for sinners and her desire to imitate Christ's sacrifice prompted her to so torment her body that, come Good Friday, her sisters feared for her survival.

Later that evening Béatrix fell into a deep slumber. Seeing her sound asleep when it came time to pray matins, her caregiver left, locking the door behind her. Shortly thereafter Béatrix awoke. She could hear the other nuns singing. Swept up in the beauty of both the chanting of her sisters and the profound meaning of the Triduum, she longed to join them.

Béatrix called for someone to open the door, but the distance and the singing rendered her cries mute. She then prayed to Our Lady truly the sweetest, most tender invocation. Next, taking a picture of the Virgin, she put it in the keyhole. The door opened, and she walked to the chapel. Seeing Béatrix shocked the sisters and caused quite a commotion. Placing her under holy obedience, the convent's chaplain and the prioress demanded she explain her presence. On hearing her story, they believed her, since no other explanation could be found.

Extreme penances weren't just for Lent; they were a constant in her life. Indeed, nothing was too severe: holding red hot coals, walking unshod in the snow, beating herself, placing her head as close as possible to a fire. She even drove dull nails through her hands in order to better experience the Passion. On these occasions clear water rather than blood came from the wounds, and when the water stopped, the wounds also disappeared.

Béatrix had apparitions and locutions from Our Lady and visions of Jesus. She heard the voice of God coming from the tabernacle, she saw the wounded Christ being carried into the convent chapel. She beheld all the saints in glory. For a long period she saw the Infant Jesus in the Host at each Mass. One Advent she abstained from Communion for fear of receiving unworthily. When she finally did take the Eucharist, the Host expanded in her throat, causing her to choke. When she coughed it up, it had become flesh.

In 1300 superiors sent her and two other religious to found a new charterhouse at Eymeux, about forty-five miles away, with Béatrix as prioress. This thrilled her, because now she could evangelize and make

Christ even more present in the world. A community quickly grew around the sisters.

Just three years later, however, Béatrix died, followed shortly by the deaths of the other foundresses. Without Béatrix's steady hand, discipline became lax. The community dissolved, and the remaining sisters returned to Parménie.

As the remains of three foundresses were still at the abandoned convent, the prioress and the chaplain at Parménie, Fr. Roz de Charis, resolved to translate them back to the motherhouse. The priest put the remains in a satchel and loaded it on his donkey. On his way back, having come across a rain-swollen river, he solicited these saints to ask God to lower the waters so he could cross over. Sure enough, the waters receded, and across he went.

Some time later, the Cathari damaged Bl. Béatrix's new tomb at Parménie, but that did absolutely nothing to stop the faithful from coming. Furthermore, great numbers who did make this pilgrimage obtained miracles. Bl. Marguerite d'Oingt says this demonstrates that Béatrix's labors pleased God even though they didn't produce permanent fruit. Perhaps the greatest miracle is that her tomb survived not only the Cathari (it was hidden and miraculously rediscovered by a shepherd in 1697) but also the French Revolution, which saw the desecration of many ancient and venerated tombs of saints.

Bl. Pius IX confirmed her cultus on April 15, 1869. The French say that if on the feast of St. Béatrix the skies are cloudy, six weeks of rain will follow.

WHY BL. BÉATRIX D'ORNACIEUX DESERVES OUR ATTENTION AND DEVOTION

Bl. Béatrix's mortifications seem at best bizarre and at worst sorely misguided. It would be a mistake, however, to get lost in such details and not see the larger example she sets for us.

She had an acute awareness of her own sins. She knew she could do nothing on her own to merit salvation. Only Jesus' sacrifice on the cross and his resurrection restored our "right" to heaven. The profundity of this filled her with gratitude, and everything she did was to show that gratitude and her contrition for sin. Maybe she was misguided, but at least she did something.

How do we manifest our love, gratitude, and respect for the price of our salvation? Do we take it for granted? Bl. Béatrix exemplified the spirit of "rejoice in God my savior" (see Luke 1:47). If we don't like her way, then let's find our own.

O Lord, your passion, death, and resurrection earned us so much. Never let us take these ineffable gifts for granted. Through Bl. Béatrix's example and prayers, give us ever-greater gratitude, zeal, and fervor and thereby make us your instruments in winning souls for you. We pray these things in your name, Lord Jesus, through the intercession of your Blessed Mother.

Bl. Giovanni della Pace

Murderous Soldier Turned Disciple of Christ

ca. 1270–ca. 1335 • Beatified: September 10, 1857

Memorial: November 12

Walk the streets of Pisa and the average citizen will gladly give you directions to that city's famous leaning tower. But ask where to find the tomb of one of their town's greatest saints, a man whose humility and holiness their ancestors once celebrated, and that person will likely say in a perplexed sort of way, "*Non conosco,*" or "I don't know."

Giovanni Cini Soldato was a native of Pisa but one you would probably avoid if you had lived at that time. He was uncouth and unpredictably violent. At the time Italy was roughly divided between the papal states and the independent city-states. The republic of Pisa was one of the latter, and Giovanni served in its army. It was in this capacity, during a civil war, that on October 8, 1296, he led an attack on a certain Matteo, the administrator general for Teodorico Ranieri, Pisa's archbishop-elect.

Found guilty of murder, Giovanni spent the next nine years in prison. It evidently gave him ample time for reflection, because on his release he had completely changed. He founded the Pious House of Mercy, which dispensed food, clothing, and cash to the impoverished. He even had night hours for those too ashamed to receive charity during the day.

Eventually Giovanni discerned a call to the eremitical life. For the rest of his days, he lived as a hermit outside Pisa's Gate of Peace, from which he took his new name, Giovanni della Pace (*pace* means "peace"). He also reestablished the Congregation of Franciscan Third Order Hermits of Penance, which had long been defunct.

Seeing the obvious joy of his humble life, many young people felt called to join him. This eventually led to the founding of the Confraternity of Disciplinati of St. John the Baptist, a large society of penitents whose church was near the Gate of Peace. Giovanni spent the rest of his life in a cell there, receiving Holy Communion through one opening and food and other alms through another. It was there that he died.

Bl. Pius IX beatified Giovanni in 1856. It is interesting that a century later a furrier and married man named Giovanni della Pace from this same city was also beatified.

WHY BL. GIOVANNI DELLA PACE DESERVES OUR ATTENTION AND DEVOTION

We see humanity's perpetual inclination toward bellicose violence in the young Giovanni, who thought nothing of attacking a clergyman of God's Holy Church. In actuality, what he attacked and wounded was the Body of Christ. We all do that whenever we sin, violently or otherwise. So Bl. Giovanni is a great role model for us, because he reminds us not only of the power of conversion but of the need for it. We can experience this as a first-time turning toward the Lord and each time we walk into the confessional.

Dear Lord Jesus, I humbly come to you and ask you to impress on my heart the ways in which I am too much like Giovanni Cino Soldato and too little like Bl. Giovanni della Pace. Make me a person of peace, love, service, repentance, penance, courage, and sacrifice. In other words, "Make my heart like unto thine."

St. Lydwine of Schiedam
She Fell to Pieces
March 18, 1380–April 14, 1433 • Canonized: March 14, 1890
Memorial: April 14

As did the Nazis, our society increasingly equates personhood with the ability to "do." If someone cannot perform basic human functions, they are counted not "fully human." However, as Benedict XVI reminds us, no matter the extent of a person's disabilities, he or she remains completely human and possesses inalienable rights endowed by the Creator. A great example of this principle is St. Lydwine (pronounced "Lid-oo-ee-nah").

Her name derives from the Flemish word *lyden*, "to suffer," and never was anyone so aptly named. Delivered on Palm Sunday in 1380, she was the only girl in a brood of nine children born to impoverished parents.

While very young, Lydwine developed a strong prayer life and a sense of piety stoked by devotion to Our Lady, as learned from her parents. One thing for which she prayed was the ability to totally belong to Our Lord. She thought this meant becoming a religious. God had other plans.

At age fourteen, on the Feast of the Purification, February 2, 1395, during a very cold winter, she and some other girls were skating on the river Maas. While horsing around, she fell and broke her rib, an injury that never healed. Eventually the pain became so intense that she couldn't get out of bed.

By 1408, Lydwine was completely paralyzed but for her neck and left hand. Soon painful bedsores covered her entire body, and these became gangrenous. Her hearing came and went. Blood poured from every opening in her head, her intestines came out, and her skin fell off. Due to a disease known as St. Anthony's Fire, eventually only a single nerve kept her right arm attached to her body. Plus she constantly had alternating bouts of extreme fever and terrible chills.

Lydwine hated this condition of hers, and she grew angry with God. It was hard to suffer the never-ending pain, her grotesque appearance, and the need for assistance required to perform every single task. She wanted to feel well and be able. She wanted a normal life again. She was a young woman who had hopes and dreams, for goodness' sake.

Her pastor, Fr. Jan Pot, taught her to meditate on the Lord's passion. Over the course of four years, she eventually accepted her situation. She learned that God's will for her was not what could or should be in the future but in the here and now, and this realization not only eased her pain but even brought her a small measure of joy. From then on, she made it her spiritual mission to join all her sufferings to the cross for the salvation of sinners and the release of souls from purgatory.

Lydwine fasted all the time, but this was more out of necessity than by choice. At first she could hold down some apple and toast, but eventually even that was too much. The only thing she could drink was water from the river Maas, and in time she acquired the ability to distinguish if it was taken when the tide was out or in. The only food she could consume without vomiting was the Eucharist, and some hagiographies say she communicated only twice a year.

As one might imagine, someone who survived only on the Eucharist caused quite a sensation. Many people thought her situation was another one of those all too common "holy hoaxes" of the time. The town burghers launched an investigation. Soldiers were charged with observing Lydwine, and they validated that she hardly ate and didn't sleep "for all the above-written seven years…except very little, and scarcely for the space of two nights, all reckoned together."[1] Besides confirming the aforementioned afflictions, they also observed grey, water-filled worms the length of half a finger that ate at her flesh.

Lydwine wasn't the only one who suffered in the small home made even more cramped by those who came to see her. Perhaps the person who suffered the most after Lydwine was her father, a night watchman who needed quiet during the day in order to sleep. And her mother had trouble being patient with her at first, but after seeing the amazing things God did through her daughter, that began to change.

Gradually, like a mature oak growing from an acorn, Lydwine developed patience by her resignation to God's will. This helped her to grow in love, not only for God but for his beautiful reflections in the souls he brought to her door. She learned to be cheerful rather than complaining and grumpy. She developed an amazing facility for prayer and even had visions. Most important is that she learned to trust God, understanding that, despite all appearances, he was in control, had a plan, and was a Father who would keep his promises. And she was happy.

After she surrendered herself to this mysterious love, Jesus gave her another gift, the stigmata. Somehow it was discovered that God gave the blood flowing from these wounds healing power. Soon a constant stream of the sick came to see Lydwine. Her intercession obtained miraculous healings for some. To others she gave special comfort and the courage to endure.

In 1425, Duke Philip of Burgundy invaded Holland. On October 10 his soldiers came to Schiedam and asked the parish priest if they could see the saint. Not suspecting anything, he agreed. Once inside Lydwine's room, the soldiers began to mock her and say disgusting things, the least of which was that her condition resulted from the priest's impregnating her.

Then the soldiers drew back the dark covering surrounding her bed. This was designed to keep out light, for her one good eye could not stand brightness. They lit a candle and held it to her face, which caused excruciating agony. Next they stripped off Lydwine's covers to have a look at her naked.

At this point her niece Petronilla had had enough, and she attacked them. The ruffians threw her against an altar in the room, which caused a permanent leg injury. They then called Lydwine a prostitute and began groping and violating her, which opened wounds in her dropsy-afflicted skin. The virgin saint began bleeding such copious amounts of blood, she filled a bowl. Soon thereafter each of these soldiers died sudden and unpleasant deaths.

Not long before her own passing, Lydwine said that if she had the chance to be healthy again, she would not take it. Through her guardian angel, God gave her the branch of a rosebush and said that when she saw it in full bloom, it would mean the end of her suffering. She saw these mature roses in a subsequent vision and died on Easter Sunday 1433 at age fifty-three.

WHY ST. LYDWINE DESERVES OUR ATTENTION AND DEVOTION

St. Lydwine proves that "human beings, irrespective of the conditions in which they live and of the capacities they are capable of expressing, possess unique and extraordinary worth from the very beginning of their existence to the moment of natural death."[2]

Dear God, the next time our leaders propose allowing euthanasia or assisted suicide, help us to understand through the prayers and the example of your servant Lydwine that we won't create a more humane, "fully human" society by killing ourselves or other humans. Furthermore, help us make such an understanding a criterion for those we choose as our leaders.

Through her intercession, help us to bear our own sufferings patiently and to offer them for your glory.

Martyrs of Otranto
The Bravehearts of Italy
d. August 14, 1480 • Beatified: October 5, 1980

Memorial: August 14

Question: What would you sacrifice for Jesus?

If you can't answer immediately, that's OK. But while you're thinking about it, consider what happened in the hot, baking summer of 1480 at Otranto, located on the heel of Italy's boot.

It was July 29, and lookouts had just spotted an armada of more than a hundred fifty ships holding eighteen thousand Muslim soldiers. Sultan Muhammad II of the Ottoman Empire had sent them to conquer the "first Rome," just as twenty-seven years before he had conquered Constantinople, the "second Rome." For three days the Ottomans had enslaved, raped, and killed Constantinople's people. Now this force would make real the dream Muhammad II had had since then: to make St. Peter's Basilica into horse stables.

Although the sultan's plan called for landing at Brindisi's easy, natural port, an ill wind forced his legion to a harbor near Otranto. Defending the city that day were just four hundred men. Seeing the huge host arrayed against them, the captain quickly realized he'd need reinforcements, and so an urgent plea went out to King Ferrante of Naples.

Meanwhile Muhammad II's commander, Gedik Ahmed Pasha, offered the Otrantini generous terms: Surrender immediately and unconditionally and everyone would go free. The city fathers promptly sent back the fifteenth-century southern-Italian version of a Bronx cheer.

The dismayed Ahmed thought that perhaps the first messenger had not properly conveyed his generous proposal, so he sent a second messenger. The archers on the city's walls used this gentleman for target practice. Just in case Ahmed hadn't gotten the message, the garrison captain climbed the ramparts' highest tower with the city's keys and hurled them into the sea.

This was a fine display of the Otrantini's bravado, but the town's experienced mercenary defenders saw no hope of victory. So one night all but fifty lowered themselves down the city walls and escaped, leaving only the residents to defend their home. With no artillery and low stores, prospects didn't look good.

For two weeks the Islamic forces ceaselessly rained down on the city a hellish hurricane of stone and burning pitch. For their part, the defenders gave as good as they got for each of those fourteen days. The citizens boiled their reserves of precious oil and water, pouring them onto their attackers.

On August 12, however, Otranto's walls weakened, and a hole opened. The invaders poured through. Slaying any who dared be on the streets along the way, they made their way to the cathedral, where they knew they would find most of the town's residents. Bursting into the building, they found Archbishop Stefano Argicolo boldly standing in the sanctuary before them, dressed in his episcopal finery, holding his crosier in one gloved hand and a crucifix in the other, as if to exorcise the intruders.

When the Muslims told the archbishop to discard the crucifix and never again utter Christ's name, he told them to convert. Then they told him…well, nothing. Instead, out came an exquisitely sharpened scimitar, and with one stroke, off came His Excellency's head. Before he collapsed, his arterial blood spilled onto the same high altar that daily saw another type of sacrifice, one that also prominently featured blood. Then they sawed in half Bishop Stefano Pendinelli and the garrison's commander, Count Francesco Zurlo. The crowning touch of this martyrdom and defilement was to execute all the attending priests and turn the cathedral into a stable.

The next day the Ottomans sent upward of five thousand able-bodied women, children, and elderly to Albania to live in slavery; the weaker ones they slaughtered. Ahmed then had all males over age fifteen—about eight hundred strong—brought before an apostate priest named Giovanni da Calabria, who exhorted them to become Muslims if they wanted to save their lives and their possessions.

One man bravely answered, an elderly tailor named Antonio Pezzulla, better known as Primaldo, for being the first *(prima)* killed. He called the apostate's suggestion insulting. On the prisoners' behalf he proclaimed their belief in God the Son and their wish that they could die for him a thousand times. Then, turning to his neighbors, he exhorted them, "Now it is time for us to fight to save our souls for Our Lord. And since he died on the cross for us, it is fitting we should die for him."[1] This elicited thunderous cheers.

The next morning the Muslims led the men to a nearby hill. Each received one more chance, and each told Ahmed no. The jihadists made Antonio the first to die because he wouldn't stop exhorting his companions to remain resolute for Christ. Kneeling before the chopping block, he shouted that he saw heavenly angel choirs waiting to receive them.

After the executioner's scimitar removed Antonio's head, a strange thing happened: His body stood and, despite the soldiers' efforts to remove it, remained fixed in place until the last man's execution. The martyrs' resolve moved one Turk to convert, and he, too, perished. While it wasn't the first time a city had to mount a defense of its Christian faith, it was the first and only time an entire municipality underwent martyrdom.

The martyrs' resistance bought King Ferrante two weeks' time to move his forces into place. This prevented the Muslims from moving up the peninsula, although they held Otranto for another year. Muhammad II had died four months before the city's recapture, and so the Basilica of St. Peter remained as it has always been, the heart of Christendom.

**WHY THE MARTYRS OF OTRANTO DESERVE OUR
ATTENTION AND DEVOTION**

What these martyrs experienced finds a depressing echo in our own headlines. So, yes, we recall them because of their bravery and heroism. More than this, though, they died precisely because they were not simply Otrantini but Christians. They knew that Jesus isn't merely another prophet of Islam but God incarnate. To have denied this would have meant living a lie. They help us to consider our own commitment to Christ and to ponder what our response would be in similar circumstances.

Lord Jesus, these men died rather than deny you. Is our zeal equal to theirs? You gave your life so that we might live. What would we give up for you? Sweet Jesus, show us our hearts as your Sacred Heart, punctured for love of us, sees them.

Bl. José de Anchieta

Patron of the New Evangelization?

March 19, 1534–June 9, 1597 • Beatified: June 22, 1980

Memorial: June 9

In the movie *The Mission*, actor Jeremy Irons plays a tall, virile, handsome priest who leads the Jesuits' efforts to convert and protect Brazilian Indians against the brutality of Portuguese colonists. Were the movie more true to life, the hero would be played by a somewhat homely nearhunchback. In short, he would have played Bl. José de Anchieta.

The son of a wealthy Spanish nobleman, Anchieta was an exceptionally brilliant student. He was also a pious boy who undertook tremendously austere mortifications, which made him weak and led to a severe spine deformation. Having discerned his priestly vocation early, he was only nineteen years old when his superiors sent him as a missionary to Brazil. They hoped the climate would help his back to heal. Sadly, it did not, and he suffered with this ailment all his life.

Along with Fr. Manuel da Nóbrega, S.J., Bl. José founded São Paulo, Rio de Janeiro, and several other towns. But more important than these settlements were the ways he initiated of interacting with the natives. He thereby succeeded in bringing many people to Christ, sometimes whole tribes.

One particularly effective method of evangelization was his writing. For instance, in the language of the Tupi Indians he wrote a play that taught them Christian morality. He also wrote stories, catechisms, and poems. His genius, one observer noted, was that he

always kept his audience firmly in mind. [For instance, in] his plays ("autos"), Anchieta used various strategies to convert the Indians and to keep the Portuguese colonists on the straight and narrow path to heaven. Anchieta's "autos" seem to include something for everyone and contain all the popular culture forms—farce, music, dance, poetic recitation, and most of all, pure spectacle.... Anchieta wanted both to amuse and instruct his diverse audience.

During his captivity by a hostile tribe, he wrote a poem of forty-nine hundred lines to Our Lady, a feat in and of itself. Making it even more impressive was that he lacked any writing materials. Every day he would trace the lines in the sand, memorize those, and then create more the next day. On his release he transcribed the whole thing. Because of his skill with words, he is considered the founder of Brazilian letters.

The good Jesuit, however, was not content with simply converting Indians. He really loved them. When the colonists tried to enslave them, Anchieta came to their defense. To put it mildly, his fellow Europeans hated him.

He also defended the natives from enemies in the wild. Just as St. Anthony preached to fish, Bl. José preached to a jaguar he and some Indians encountered in the jungle. The animal grew calm and walked away, which is why people invoke Bl. José's intercession against animal attacks.

Somehow Fr. José learned to practice medicine, and he lovingly healed many Indians. When he died at Reritiba, three thousand of them turned out to mourn him.

WHY BL. JOSÉ DE ANCHIETA DESERVES OUR ATTENTION AND DEVOTION

We often think of those who formally serve God simply as preachers, sacrament dispensers, and so on. Bl. José did all of that and more. He helped found a nation. He left a mark people remember and revere to this day.

Each of us has abilities we can use for God. Whether it be working on our personal sanctity or trying to make this world a better place by spreading the gospel, each of us can do something that will leave a mark. It's not too late. You're still breathing. What is God calling you to do?

Dear Lord Jesus, you gave your servant José the grace to spread your gospel in innovative ways. You also helped him love and defend the defenseless. Help us to follow, out of love for you, his example in all things.

Bl. Sebastián de Aparicio

The First Cowboy

January 20, 1502–February 25, 1600 • Beatified: May 17, 1789

Memorial: February 25

In 1 Corinthians 12:4–11, St. Paul writes that the Holy Spirit gave each of us a gift and that we are to use it for the common good. Although he is forgotten, Bl. Sebastián of Aparicio is nonetheless one of the Church's best examples of this ever. His story can help us to discern our gift and how God wants us to use it.

Born in Spain, Sebastián was the only son of a moderately impoverished farming family. His father, Juan, was a good farmer and a master ox tamer.

As a youth Sebastián sometimes went to Puerto Castilla to find work when the family needed extra income. Seeing the bright lights and big city, and hearing numerous stories of easily made fortunes in New Spain, the fifteen-year-old yearned to leave farm life. His parents, however, refused. He was their only son; who would take over if his father died or was injured? They finally relented, provided he first earn dowries for his two sisters. And so in 1533, at age thirty-one, he finally emigrated to New Spain, ultimately settling at Puebla, the first wholly colonial city in Mexico.

At first, he tried farming. However, despite his having made the first plow in the New World, he had no success. Always one to sense opportunity, though, he identified a problem and found a solution.

Before the Spaniards arrived, the Americas had few oxen or horses. Then the Spaniards imported so many that their numbers became unmanageable, and most became feral. The colonists needed someone to rustle up the livestock, which Sebastián knew how to do. Then he could train the animals to pull a cart. This is how Sebastián became the first cowboy in the Americas.

The next opportunity he seized came about because all cargo going to Mexico City from Veracruz—the colony's only port—had to pass through Puebla. To get to and from Mexico City, it was hauled on people's backs via time-worn paths. Noting to royal officials the obvious problem with this and proposing for them the evident solution, Sebastián offered himself as the best man for the job. Thus, within a few months, Sebastián had built nice, level roads between Puebla and the two cities. Then for the next few years, he was essentially a trucker, transporting passengers and goods. He obtained the postal concession as well.

All of this made him very wealthy and a major landowner. He had obtained his dream. Sebastián then shared shared his good fortune with others by starting schools so that the natives could learn the trade skills required by the Spaniards. He built them homes and gave them food and clothing.

In 1542, Sebastián moved to Mexico City to exploit the greater opportunities waiting there for a savvy businessman. This change in scenery paid off—and handsomely—because he soon won the contract to build the first road between the capital and the silver mines at Zacatecas, 336 miles away. What's more, for ten years he had exclusive rights to transport silver ore between the two cities. He also transported passengers.

These journeys often took him through areas controlled by the Chichimecas, a tribe of Indians so feared that even the other indigenous peoples called them savages. Not once, however, did they molest Sebastián, because he won them over with his charity, kindness, and obvious goodwill. Whereas others rocketed through their territory with the sort of unrelenting fear that resulted in the involuntary relaxation of their bladders, the Chichimecas always greeted Sebastián's approach with warmth and hospitality.

That isn't to say he never encountered trouble, though. One time, as he pulled into Mexico City's Zócalo, a crockery vendor drew his sword and attacked his goods, smashing them on the pavement. Like a sixteenth-century John Wayne, Sebastián jumped off his cart, threw the man to the ground, disarmed him, dug his knee into his chest, and ever so persuasively pressed the sharp point of the man's own sword to the tip of his nose. The man apologized for the love of God, and at that Sebastián helped him to his feet, saying the two were now friends.

After eighteen years on the road, the fifty-year-old Sebastian decided to retire and become a cattle rancher. Retirement's slow pace allowed him to notice the poverty all around him, especially that of the Indians. He began to give away more and more of his wealth. He gave food and drink to all who called and rooms to pilgrims on their way to the Guadalupe shrine.

Sebastián also started teaching Indians the trades again. Additionally, he paid their outstanding debts, and he learned their language so that he could help them in their effort to learn their catechism. He slept as they did, on floor mats of woven reeds. His diet was their diet, corn tortillas with chilies. While he wasn't poor, he was most certainly poor in spirit.

Some years later his many head of cattle in Chapultepec required his presence, so he moved to the town and promptly contracted a disease serious enough that he received last rites. Following his recovery, his friends encouraged him to marry, even though he was now sixty.

Now, women had always found Sebastián incredibly handsome. The less virtuous ladies even propositioned him. He never gave in to these temptations. He had remained chaste.

After much prayer and discernment, he decided his friends were right so he married the daughter of a neighbor. She died a year later, however. Two years later he married another young woman, but she died after only eight months following her fall from a tree during the harvesting of their ranch's fruit. Was God trying to tell him something?

He again became ill—so ill, in fact, that he made out his will. He recovered, however, and started spending more and more time in prayer in church. In doing so, he increasingly felt attracted to the religious life.

He couldn't determine, however, whether this was the best move for him. Was it God's will? To test his vocation, Sebastián's spiritual director sent him to work as a servant in a local Poor Clares convent. Imagine seeing one of your country's wealthiest citizens serving as a domestic, and you have some idea of how shocked this left many people. Yet this was the happiest he had ever been. The reason for this is that he was finally acting in accord with his deepest and most persistent longings.

Having confirmed his vocation, Sebastián became a Franciscan novice in 1574 at the convent of San Francisco in Mexico City. When they took him in, the Franciscans probably thought he wouldn't be with them long, given his advanced age. Yet he worked just as hard as someone in his early twenties and always with the attitude that he was the luckiest guy in the world.

However, his wasn't all a bed of roses. For the first time since leaving Spain, he had to live in community. It was a difficult adjustment. Making it worse were the younger friars. They didn't know his background, so they made fun of this "old man." They had open debates about whether he was too old to be a Franciscan. Compounding this, it is said that Satan sent him temptations that had never before bothered him. Sebastián felt a little dejected.

Then one night in a dream, St. Francis of Assisi and St. James, his nation's patron, spoke to him and confirmed his vocation. Not long thereafter his superiors gave him their approval. When he took his final vows, a priest had to sign for him, as he was still illiterate.

His superiors moved him to Puebla, where they gave him the job of beggar. His duties required him to travel a roughly five-hundred-mile circuit. Toward the end of a journey, this aged man would sometimes find himself terribly ill, even near death. When this happened, he prayed.

He would begin by stating the obvious: that God, knowing his servant's weakness and unworthiness, had nonetheless willed the task to him. So many depended on his efforts. He could not fail them. He would conclude by asking for the strength and ability to complete the holy mission that rested on his shoulders. Invariably, when Sebastián awoke the next morning, either he was cured or his oxen practically flew so that the journey was quickly completed.

His love for Our Lady was profound, and he grew to love praying the rosary. Once he arrived at the convent in Cholula during Mass, tired and dusty from his journeys. As he approached the Communion rail, he saw Our Lady. Sebastián became excited and shouted to the priest about her beauty. Seeing nothing, Father at first thought Fray Sebastián was crazy, but then he understood that he had had a vision.

With the good comes the bad, however, and Sebastián suffered occasional physical attacks by demons. Indeed, his provincial superior said of him, "He saw more demons than mosquitoes."[1] Once some demons threatened to throw him headlong out the window because, they said, God had told them to. Fray Sebastián tranquilly responded, "Well, then, if God has sent you for this, why do you wait? Do whatever he sends you to do. I am very happy to do what is pleasing to God."[2]

From all the riding he did, he developed a hernia, which never had time to heal because he was always out on the road doing his job as a beggar. On February 20, 1600, returning from Tlaxcala, the pain became so intense that he began to vomit, and he barely made it home to Puebla. For five days he refused his bed and lay prostrate on the floor before the Blessed Sacrament.

Finally, on February 25, 1600, this incredible man, who despite his illiteracy had accomplished so much, breathed his last. It took four days for all those paying their respects to file past his funeral bier. Beatified in 1789 by Pope Clement XIII, Bl. Sebastián has nearly a thousand miracles attributed to his intercession. His incorrupt remains repose in a glass coffin in Puebla's San Francisco Church.

WHY BL. SEBASTIÁN DESERVES OUR ATTENTION AND DEVOTION

At every turn Bl. Sebastián used his abilities to accomplish something good. Through his charity and concern for others, he gave back to God the fruits he had received. Are we doing the same?

Lord Jesus, you told us the parable of the talents, as a warning not to let our gifts go unused (see Matthew 25:14–30). Through the intercession of Bl. Sebastián, help us to properly discern those talents you have given us. Then show us how you want us to use those, not only in ways proper to our vocation but in service to your Church and our fellow man as well.

St. Lorenzo Ruiz

A Boat to Martyrdom

ca. 1600–September 29, 1637 • Canonized: October 18, 1987

Memorial: September 28

Imagine being your household's sole support and one day someone approaches you at gunpoint and says, "Your faith or your life." How do you respond? That is the dilemma faced by St. Lorenzo Ruiz, a husband and father, and his answer gives us much to consider.

Born near Manila, his mother was Filipino and his father Chinese, and both were devout converts. His father was likely an artisan whose skills the Spaniards needed as they built their colony. However, the Spaniards also looked on with him suspicion, since Chinese immigrants had attempted a revolt in the years surrounding Lorenzo's birth. And so, even though Lorenzo was officially a *mestizo de sangley* (mixed Chinese-Filipino), he always said he was Filipino.

He studied at the local Dominican school, where he learned calligraphy and Spanish. These skills enabled him to get work both as a secretary at the local parish and with the government, for which he translated documents from the local dialect into Spanish. That is how he supported his wife, two sons, and daughter.

Lorenzo also profited from the Dominicans' love for knowledge. He really knew his catechism and was an active, committed Catholic. Besides being an altar server, he was a sacristan and a member of the Confraternity of the Holy Rosary. All of this made him a valuable asset to his community.

In 1636, however, Lorenzo was implicated in the murder of a Spaniard with whom he had feuded. Authorities weren't sure if he was a suspect or merely knew about the crime, so they issued an arrest warrant. Because he was a mestizo, he doubted whether the Spaniards would treat him justly. Knowing some priests were leaving the country, he asked to join them. And so he and three Dominican priests boarded a ship that he thought was headed for Macau, a Portuguese colony in China, but was actually going to Japan.

When the boat landed at Okinawa, the Japanese arrested the men immediately for the crime of being Christians. Christianity had recently become illegal in Japan, and the government had unleashed a hellish persecution. On July 10, 1636, exactly a month after their leaving the Philippines, their captors took them to Nagasaki, where the four men endured truly hideous tortures. Their jailers would force huge quantities of water down their throats. Then, when their bellies were painfully and grotesquely extended, the jailers would place wide boards across their stomachs and step or jump on these, so that the liquid would come stinging out of the mouth, nose, and ears. They also put needles under the men's fingernails and subjected them to beatings.

The authorities offered Lorenzo freedom if he apostatized. He almost did because of the extreme makeover (torture edition) he had received. However, through what must have been an incredible infusion of God's grace, Lorenzo not only reconsidered, he grew ever bolder. He told his torturers, "I am a Christian, and this I profess until the hour of my death, and for God, I shall give my life. Although I did not come to Japan to be a martyr, nevertheless, as a Christian and for God, I shall give my life."[1]

A year later, on September 27, 1637, his captors led Lorenzo and fifteen companions to Nishizaka Hill, the "Mountain of Martyrs." Although in agony, in his loudest voice he told bystanders what he had told the judges: "I am a Christian, and I shall die for God, and for Him I would give many thousands of lives if I had them."[2]

Then his captors hanged him and the other four faithful upside down, with boards fitted around their waists, and topped these with rock weights, their heads hanging down into a pit. This caused an excruciatingly painful, creeping death, and indeed, it took Lorenzo and the leper St. Lazaro of Kyoto two days to expire. On the third day their companions, Sts. Vicente Shiwozuka de la Cruz, Guillermo Courtet, and Miguel de Aozaraza, all Dominican priests, all somehow still clung to life, so they were cut down and beheaded. The emperor then had their remains cremated and their ashes scattered.

Lorenzo was no older than thirty-seven at his death. In 1987, Bl. Pope John Paul II made him the first Filipino saint and martyr.

WHY ST. LORENZO RUIZ DESERVES OUR ATTENTION AND DEVOTION
For those with families to support, making the choice St. Lorenzo did is horrifying to contemplate. But while we don't face torture and execution, doesn't life give us scores of similar choices? It does. Each day gives us *many* opportunities to die to ourselves by giving witness to our faith.

Hardly any of us want to do that, though, do we? After all, think of what that might cost us. At the very least, it might cost us human respect. But it could also cost us even more: friends, family, standing in the community, jobs.

What if we don't share our faith, though? What might *that* cost us? What might it cost others? After all, isn't our hoped-for salvation God's greatest gift to us? Shouldn't we want to share that with others? Don't we want them to have the very thing for which St. Lorenzo was ready to "give many thousands of lives if [he] had them"? How can we keep something that fantastic from others?

Because doing so is tough, that's how. Well, like us, St. Lorenzo had every earthly reason to not do what he did. He was not even supposed to be in Japan, for goodness' sake.

He knew, however, that our salvation is our most precious gift, and he was not about to jeopardize that for anything in the world.

Therefore, be bold like St. Lorenzo. Be not afraid, like St. Lorenzo. Step out of the boat and onto the water, like St. Lorenzo. Because no matter what it costs, heaven is worth it, both for us and the souls we touch.

Lord, you told us, "Whoever denies me before men, I also will deny before my Father who is in heaven" (Matthew 10:33). We have jobs, though, families, friends. What will we do if our faith costs us these?

Trusting you is easy in thought. Actually doing so is another matter. Through St. Lorenzo's example and prayers, build our trust to be like a strong muscle so that we will never deny you. Through Mary's intercession, help us to remember that the rewards you give for faithfulness far outweigh the costs.

St. Pedro de San José Betancur

Not Smart Enough to Be a Priest

March 21, 1626–April 25, 1667 • Canonized: July 30, 2002

Memorial: April 18

Sometimes in life we repeatedly try to get through a door that just won't budge. Then we move to another that not only easily opens, but it takes us to the same place we wanted to go in the first place. If you've known that sort of experience, you know something of our next saint.

Born on Tenerife, one of Spain's Canary Islands, St. Pedro of St. Joseph herded his family's sheep. While in the fields, he often passed the time in prayer and thinking of God. He would stick his staff in the ground and use it as a sundial so he would know when to begin his eucharistic fast before Mass. To mortify his flesh, he ate only bread and water four days a week. When he wasn't praying, or sometimes when he was, he'd daydream, usually about the news reaching his home from the West Indies.

The time came when his widowed mother wanted him to marry a local girl. However, he had already decided to devote his life to God (proving that even saints don't talk with their mothers as much as they should). Living on the remote Canary Islands, however, how would he do that?

An especially pious aunt, known for her unique ability to discern God's will, told him to go to the New World. An old man on the island independently told him the same thing. So on September 18, 1649, at the age of twenty-three, he left his home for good.

Evidently he underestimated the amount of money required for the trip, because when he reached Havana, he had none. He took work as a weaver there and earned enough to resume his journey after a year. The ship dropped him at Trujillo, Honduras. There he heard about Guatemala for the first time and immediately set out for that westward land. On his arrival on February 18, 1651, he knelt and kissed the ground, at which point an earthquake occurred.

It was exciting to be in Guatemala, but once again he hadn't budgeted for his journey and was literally starving. In desperation he visited a Franciscan bread dispensary. It took the friars one look to see how sick he was, so they admitted him into one of their hospices. During his convalescence there, he saw people who were even more destitute than he. It got him thinking about how to help these poor people.

When a wealthy distant relation learned Pedro was at the hospital, he took him to live in his beautiful home. Not needing to work for the time being, the young man spent his days visiting San Francisco Church, where he met and took as his confessor the native Guatemalan priest, Fr. Fernando Espino, o.f.m. The friar convinced him to leave his relative's luxurious home and move into the Franciscans' upper cloister.

Now he needed a job, and so in Lent 1651 Pedro took a job as an entry-level weaver, where he became friends with the factory owner's son. This man gave him good books to read, which helped Pedro improve his reading, writing, and knowledge of the faith.

What he read in these books increased his zeal. And so bit by bit, he began taking on more and more penances. He would fast from noon Thursday until noon Saturday. Late on Thursday and Friday nights, he would take a heavy wooden cross and carry it to the city's Calvary Chapel. He also joined many lay associations.

All of this made him the object of both admiration and scorn. He was especially mocked by four convicts working off their sentences in the factory. His example and words, though, ultimately convinced at least two to accept Christ.

Through such experiences and much prayer, Pedro discerned a vocation to the priesthood, and he entered the Jesuit seminary. Between his factory work, studies, and charitable work, however, he hardly ever slept, and he made horrible grades. Then he lost his job because he refused a marriage match attempted by his boss, who didn't realize that Pedro wanted to be a priest. By God's grace a well-off man agreed to fund Pedro's schooling. Even so, he made no progress and had to drop out of the seminary.

What would he do now? He prayed and made a pilgrimage to the Shrine of Our Lady of Good Help in Petapa, with the intention that the Blessed Virgin would help him know her Son's will. But after an all-day vigil there, he had no better sense of where God wanted him.

On his return home, however, he ran into a man who also came from Tenerife and and who wanted to meet Pedro. This man suggested that Pedro join the tertiary Franciscans. As if to confirm that this was God's will for him, on returning to the city, Fr. Espino offered him the tertiary's habit. Not surprisingly, Pedro could not afford it, so a local knight bought it for him.

Hermano (Brother) Pedro took his initial vows on July 8, 1656. Within two weeks he who once struggled with seminary studies had memorized the entire twenty-plus–chapter Rule of St. Francis. Maybe God had put up an insurmountable roadblock at the seminary to help Pedro more perfectly follow his will.

He lived at Calvary Chapel, taking care of the grounds, and for him this was paradise. But when visiting town, his heart broke over all the destitute people he saw. One day an old black man approached him at the chapel and said, "God did not bring you here solely to take care of Calvary. Go. Get out of here. There are many poor and needy through whom you can serve God, and you will benefit both yourself and them."[1]

So he set about trying to be another Christ to the poor in his humility, poverty, penance, and service. He ministered to the sick, imprisoned, unemployed, and youth. Hermano Pedro called this work "Bethlehem," recalling the poverty of Jesus' first home on earth, and he called the hospital for the poor he later opened Our Lady of Bethlehem. This was followed by a homeless shelter, a school for poor children, and an inn for priests. All of this was done by a simple Franciscan who had no money. God simply took care of him.

Hermano Pedro was ahead of the times in using new teaching methods and in establishing social services previously unimaginable. Soon others joined him in his work, and so he wrote up a rule. The women teachers adopted it as their own and formed a religious order with his help.

Pedro's profound devotion to Our Lady led him to popularize the rosary in Guatemala. And when Pope Alexander VII in 1661 issued a bull affirming the doctrine of the Immaculate Conception,[2] St. Pedro was delirious with joy. He was seen singing, jumping in the air, and talking to himself and God with words of exultation.

He heard Mass at least once each day, frequently received Communion, and often prayed before the tabernacle of any church he happened to pass, even if he was on his way to an appointment and this meant being late. Knowing his devotion to Our Lord in the Blessed Sacrament, the bishop appointed Hermano Pedro to lead the Corpus Christi procession. He did, and was like David dancing before the ark as it was brought into Jerusalem (see 2 Samuel 6:12–15). For two hours the saint danced and waved a pole with his mantle on it, exhorting onlookers to experience joy at Christ passing before them. The people did indeed have joy, because Hermano Pedro was so sincerely enthusiastic in his love for the Eucharist. In a poem, he wrote that because of the Eucharist he had "lost my sanity," for "I can do no more / with this mystery. And because I have lost this sanity, he gives me a remedy."[3]

Satan harassed Hermano Pedro on occasion, tempting him with arguments against the faith. Pedro simply and wisely responded that he was too stupid to understand and that Satan should take his arguments to the teachers and confessors.

St. Pedro died at the age of forty-one. His funeral was a mob scene, with swarms of people from all classes pouncing on his casket, kissing his feet, and tearing at his clothing. Had it not been for the guards around his coffin, his body would have been maimed.

Why St. Pedro de San José deserves our attention and devotion

When things don't go the way we plan, consider that God may be preventing us from going down the wrong path. Attribute everything to the will of God—his passive will or his active will, what he simply allows or what he truly desires. Then pray for the humility and grace to follow him wherever he leads. When we do this, as Hermano Pedro decisively proves, we'll get what we want in the end.

Our Father in heaven, help us follow St. Pedro's example of submission to and trust in your will, our surest path to happiness, both earthly and eternal.

Martyrs of Korea
Hope for the Church in Our Times
d. 1839, 1846, and 1867 • Canonized: May 6, 1984

Memorial: September 20

Since, well, forever, naysayers have said that the gospel will never really take root in Far East Asia. If that's true, how do we explain South Korea? Catholicism there is exploding, in part because of the rich history of the Church there.

There have been Korean Christians since the late sixteenth century. The original community of the faithful was small, however, and had no access to priests, largely because the nation's rulers kept the country isolated. Then, in 1784, while on a diplomatic mission to Beijing, Yi Seung-un obtained some Chinese-language Jesuit literature, which he brought back to Korea. The dissemination of this material led to many conversions.

The ruling Choson dynasty had been worried by the mere introduction of this foreign religion. Now with Catholicism so rapidly growing, it became alarmed.

The reason is that the official state belief system was Confucianism, and for roughly four hundred years, it had helped keep order and harmony in the Hermit Kingdom (so-called because of its isolationism). Therefore, the emperor and his officials convinced themselves Confucianism had to be the kingdom's only belief system.

However, given the mutually exclusive claims of it and Christianity, this new religion provided a frightening challenge. Throughout its history, Korea had known political factionalism all too well. This had led to bloodshed and all sorts of other problems. What would happen if religious factionalism was allowed to make things even worse?

Compounding the situation was *Ex Illa Die,* a bull that Clement XI had issued in 1715 and that Benedict XIV had affirmed in 1742. It said Catholics could not observe Confucian customs, including ancestor veneration. This was a problem for the dynasty because such veneration was a huge part of Korean culture.

For these reasons, it outlawed Christianity in 1785. Despite this, some Koreans smuggled the Chinese Catholic priest Fr. Zhou Wenmo into the country in 1795. This made him the first Catholic cleric to ever set foot on Korean soil. Imagine his surprise upon learning that the Korean Church already had four thousand believers. This was a tremendous achievement, considering that the community had been completely lay-led. Such a thing had never happened in the Church's history.

In any event, by the time Fr. Zhou gave his martyrdom in a small persecution seven years later, the Church had grown to ten thousand members. Over the next thirty-five years, political factionalism kept persecutions sporadic and often regionalized. This relative freedom allowed the Church to make more converts. With the introduction of French missionaries in 1835, thousands more still became Christians.

Near the decade's end, however, the government no longer contented itself with half measures. This is how the faithful came to suffer terrible persecutions in the years 1839, 1846, and 1867, with most martyrs being laymen.

The most famous of these is St. Andrew Kim Taegon, the first native Korean priest. Born in 1821 to noble parents who were among the first converts (his father is Bl. Ignatius Kim), Andrew was baptized at age fifteen. Shortly thereafter, he traveled thirteen hundred miles to attend seminary in the then-Portuguese colony of Macao and received ordination to the priesthood in Shanghai nine years later.

Given that Christianity was illegal, Fr. Kim had to sneak back into his country. Nearly nine months later, on September 16, 1846, he was arrested for "communication with foreigners" (that is, smuggling foreign priests into the country) and beheaded near Seoul.

"This is my last hour of life, listen to me attentively," he told his executioners. "Become Christians if you wish to be happy after death, because God has eternal chastisements in store for those who have refused to know Him."[1]

In the face of such persecution, one can easily understand how the numbers of Korean Catholics had dwindled to a little over thirteen thousand souls by the time they achieved emancipation in 1883. Since then, however, the Church in South Korea has grown to 5.1 million Catholics (over 10 percent of the population), and it has produced the fourth-largest number of saints by nation.

WHY THE KOREAN MARTYRS DESERVE OUR ATTENTION AND DEVOTION:

In 1998 the Republic of Korea elected its first Catholic president, Kim Dae Jung. When Cardinal Stephen Kim of Seoul died in 2009, the entire nation mourned. Several recent opinion polls show that the Catholic Church is the most respected institution in the land. As such, the Church in Korea is proof that the gospel can take root and flourish anywhere.

Holy Spirit, you stir the hearts of men and enkindle in them the fire of your love, regardless of borders, ethnicity, or race. Unite all peoples everywhere in your one, holy, Catholic, apostolic Church, so that they may have the greatest means possible to attain salvation. Then, on that rock of Peter, let us build a civilization of charity, friendship, and goodwill. In Jesus' name we pray.

St. Charles Lwanga and Companions

**Martyrs for the Authentic Understanding
of the Human Person**

d. June 3, 1886 • Canonized: October 18, 1964

Memorial: June 3

In his Letter to the Romans, St. Paul describes how cultural degradation enables people to believe good is bad and vice versa (see Romans 1:18–32). Isaiah previously showed that this mind-set will bring anything but happiness and success (see Isaiah 5:20–25). And yet, doesn't this at least partly describe our own times?

For instance, before the turn of the century, support for marriage alternatives was scant. Before 1930 not a single Christian denomination on the planet said contraception was acceptable. And before 1970, abortion was rightly seen by many as murder.

Today, however, laws force even religious employers to provide contraception coverage in their employees' health-insurance plans. Nurses lose their jobs if they refuse to assist at abortions. Opponents of same-sex unions have been denied entrance into master's programs, lost employment, and been sued for discrimination. Upholding what for nearly two thousand years have been universally held moral truths can get us in real trouble.

So we live in bewildering times. How do we react? Hopefully as St. Charles Lwanga and his fellow Ugandan martyrs did. Among the first Christians in Uganda, through their fidelity to the gospel they stand out as a great example for all of us.

In the early 1870s, King Mutesa had given Catholic missionaries free reign to preach the faith throughout the country. However, his prime minister, or *katikiro*, despised the Christians and conspired to kill them. Hearing of this, the missionaries quickly baptized the newly converted and escaped with as many as could follow.

On Mutesa's death, his eighteen-year-old son, Mwanga II, succeeded him. As he had high regard for "the praying ones," he invited the missionaries back. Unfortunately, Mwanga was a pederast with a fondness for the young pages in his court, many of whom were Christians.

Joseph Mukasa, majordomo for Mwanga and a Christian, hid many of the youth, which irritated the king. When Mwanga had an Anglican missionary killed for opposing his lust, Joseph chastised him. This made Mwanga livid, and he ordered Joseph's execution.

As the soldiers manhandled him on his arrest, Joseph exclaimed, "I am going to die for my religion. You need not be afraid that I will attempt to escape. A Christian who gives his life for God has no reason to fear death."[1] His last words were, "Tell the King I gladly pardon him for killing me without reason, but that I advise him to repent. If not, I shall act as his accuser before the judgment seat of God."[2]

Awed by the courage Joseph's religious faith gave him, many Ugandans desired instruction and baptism. Among these were Charles Lwanga, the man who took Joseph's place as majordomo, and many of the pages.

Until they became Christians, King Mwanga had enjoyed free rein with these boys. Now they rebuffed his advances, which infuriated him. He called for St. Dennis Sebuggwawo, the Christian pages' catechist. When he appeared, Mwanga drove a spear through his neck. Dennis endured extreme pain for two days before his death, all the while praying for the king's soul.

The king resolved to kill all the Christians in his court. He assembled his pages and courtiers to discover which were Christians. Knowing beforehand the king was planning to do this, Charles and his companions prayed for the strength to suffer as Jesus had: freely, holding nothing back, and for the love of souls. Charles then gave the sacrament of baptism to those who had not yet received it.

When all had presented themselves to Mwanga, he ordered the Christians to separate from the others. Charles, taking the hand of the young catechumen Kizito, was the first to do so. The others followed. The chief executioner saw his son Mbaga Tuzinde in the group. The father ordered and finally begged him to leave, but Mbaga merely replied, "My true father, whom I must obey before all, is in heaven."[3] Standing next to the king was one of the bodyguards, Bruno Serunkuma. He, too, took his place among the condemned faithful. When Pontian Ngondwe, the man in charge of growing the king's bananas, begged to immediately join these future saints, the guards gave him a head start, slicing a machete down the length of his body and decapitating him.

The twenty-six prisoners were marched to Namugongo, thirty-seven miles away. On the way there, executioners hacked one to death. They drove a spear through another because his constricting leg irons rendered him unable to walk. He made no sound.

As they came to each crossroads they killed a prisoner as an example to others, and at one, Athanasius Bazzekuketta, twenty, volunteered. Bruno was the next to die. He was severely beaten. Recalling Christ's example on the cross, he refused the banana wine offered him.

Then the *katikiro* demanded that the death of district judge Matthias Kalemba be more terrible than the rest. The evil man taunted him, asking whether his God would save him. Matthias said quietly, "God will rescue me. But you will not see how he does it, because he will take my soul and leave you only my body."[4]

The executioners hacked off his arms and legs and burned them before his eyes. They then tied his arteries and threw him in a field to die in the scorching African sun.

Finally arriving at Namugongo, the executioners began killing the remaining prisoners one after the other. Senkole had a grudge against Charles Lwanga. Coming to him, Senkole said, "This one is of my own selection for torture."[5]

"I am happy to die for the true faith," said Charles. Turning to his brothers, he said, "My friends, we shall before long meet again in heaven."[6] Put on a funeral pyre, Charles continued praying as the fire slowly licked his body. Lovingly he said to Senkole, "How happy I would be if you embraced my religion."[7]

The executioners bound the remaining Christians inside reed mats and lit them. One brave soul called out, "Tell *Mapera* [Ugandan for "priest"] that we were faithful!"

Later, recalling the blood and ashes that littered the sub-Saharan ground that day, one executioner stated, "We have put many people to death, but never such as these. [Other] victims did nothing but moan and weep,...but the Christians...prayed until they died."[8]

It is said that the blood of the martyrs is the seed of Christianity, which is now Uganda's largest religion. Indeed, 41.9 percent of the country's thirty-two million people are Catholic, and St. Mary Cathedral in Rubaga was built over the palace of King Mwanga. For his part, Mwanga died on the Seychelles Islands, a prisoner of the British and a baptized Anglican convert.

WHY ST. CHARLES LWANGA AND COMPANIONS DESERVE OUR ATTENTION AND DEVOTION

Since the birth of Christianity, every age to one degree or another has detested the Church's call to a moral life. People have the notion that the Church wants to suffocate their freedom. Since these people can't understand how our faith actually leads us to a true freedom that in turn would bless them with a happy life, they attack the Church's teachings. Additionally, many believe if they can show that the Church is wrong on these points, they can discredit her in so much else as well.

What happened in Uganda was not just an attack on men; it was an attack on the exclusive dignity of spousal love and thereby an attack on both the gospel and the Church's very existence. And yet that attack at Namugongo failed: Today some four hundred million Africans call themselves Christian. The attack will fail elsewhere as well. It always has.

Lord Jesus, more than ever the world today hates the fullness of your gospel, and it hates your Church for protecting it. Sometimes this hatred is ferocious. In its face, help us to not be afraid. Your sacred name is all-powerful, and while Satan "prowls around like a roaring lion, seeking some one to devour" (1 Peter 5:8), you alone defeated death. With you on our side, whom have we to fear (see Isaiah 41:10–12)?

St. Mary Helen MacKillop

The Excommunicated Saint

January 15, 1842–August 8, 1909 • Canonized: October 17, 2010

Memorial: August 8

In our times obedience to authority has become an unbearable vice, whereas doing your own thing, dissent, and disobedience are the "spirit" of the greatest virtue. With that in mind, consider the story of St. Mary Helen MacKillop.

She was the first of eight children born to immigrant parents in Fitzroy, Australia. Although he was a loving, hardworking husband and father, her dad, Alexander, was never successful in any field, and it seems he tried them all. Usually he was absent, seeking the next great opportunity. This explains in part why the MacKillops' was an unsettled, unhappy home—that is, when there was a home, as their poor circumstances prompted many moves.

The family made ends meet on small jobs done by the children. This work especially fell on Mary, the eldest. This is how in 1860 she came to be governess for her wealthy aunt and uncle. She also cared for the poor children on the estate. Two years later she took a teaching job in Portland, Victoria. She did well enough to open her own boarding school in 1864, which she named Bay View House Seminary for Young Ladies.

While tutoring her cousins, Mary met Fr. Julian Tenison Woods. He became her spiritual director, and they discussed her heart's longing to find more ways to help the poor. This meshed with Father's own concerns for the area's many immigrants and especially with his concerns about their lack of Catholic education. Seeing the quality of Mary's work, he asked her and her two sisters to start a Catholic school in 1866. This opened a short while later in a stable her brother John renovated to fit their needs.

Since John was old enough to be the family's primary support, Mary decided it was time to follow her heart's desire and become a consecrated virgin. Beginning on the feast of St. Joseph in 1866, she began dressing only in black. On the feast of the Assumption the following year, she took her formal vows and founded the Sisters of St. Joseph of the Sacred Heart, becoming the mother superior and adopting the name Sr. Mary of the Cross. While Fr. Woods had suggested her name, she decided on it because she saw the cross as a tremendous blessing in spiritual growth.

The Sisters of St. Joseph of the Sacred Heart were the first Australian religious order. They wore a brown habit, which led to the sisters' nickname, "the Brown Joeys," although they were officially called the Josephites. Fr. Woods wrote their rule, which asserted that divine providence would supply everything. It also stipulated that the sisters would go wherever needed and would renounce all personal property and live in poverty.

By the end of the first year, the order had attracted ten other women, including Mary's sister Lexie. Within two years they had seventy sisters teaching in twenty-one schools throughout the country. By 1871, just four years after their founding, the Josephites had 130 women working in forty schools and other ministries.

All of the order's schools were unique in that they accepted any child regardless of the parents' ability to pay tuition. In addition to the three Rs, students learned practical things like the proper way to write a letter and how to calculate a grocery bill. They were also given a strong foundation in the faith.

Many of the schools sprouted in new farming towns, where the sisters, whose average age was just twenty-three, shared all the hardships of their fellow settlers. To encourage the sisters, especially in their spiritual life, Mary wrote each one regularly. The sisters branched out to orphanages, the care of neglected children and girls who would have otherwise turned to prostitution, and the care of seniors and those with chronic and terminal illnesses.

Much of this work centered in Adelaide, situated at the south central tip of the country and today Australia's fifth-largest city. During the order's first few years, the bishop of the diocese was Laurence Sheil, who for much of that time was too infirm to lead. The power vacuum this created gave rise to bitter disputes between various clergy and lay factions.

Bishop Sheil's appointment to oversee education was Fr. Woods, and he was becoming something of a cross for everyone. Sr. Mary actually had to return home from establishing a foundation in Brisbane because the Adelaide sisters doubted Fr. Woods's ability to lead them.

Certain clerical factions clashed with Woods because of how he wanted them to run parochial schools. They therefore sought to discredit him by discrediting the Josephites. That it was not uncommon to see the sisters begging in the streets for their sustenance led to rumors of fiscal mismanagement.

The biggest ammunition against the Brown Joeys, however, came from their trying to do the right thing. In a situation too painfully familiar to us today, allegations surfaced that a certain Fr. Keating had abused children in his care. The sisters told Fr. Woods, who reported this to Fr. John Smyth, the vicar general, who in turn sent Keating back to Ireland. The official line was that he had an alcohol problem.

This action infuriated his friend Fr. Charles Horan. He swore vengeance on Fr. Woods and the Josephites. When Fr. Smyth died in 1870, Fr. Horan became vicar general, and this gave him leverage to persuade the bishop that the true force for evil in the diocese was the Josephites. He told His Excellency that if the sisters didn't immediately change their rule, they would spin out of control, and who knew where that would lead? The bishop acquiesced.

When Sr. Mary was told to give her consent, however, she refused. This was more than Fr. Horan could have hoped for. Her stance allowed him to obtain her excommunication for insubordination. It was an old-fashioned excommunication, too. She was to be shunned, declared anathema (see 1 Corinthians 5:11-13 and Matthew 18:15). In other words, she could have no contact with any Catholic, and no Catholic could have contact with her. She removed her habit and went to live with a Jewish family.

Now, Sr. Mary was not excommunicated for uncovering sex abuse, as some news outlets have salaciously reported. When the Keating incident happened, she was in Queensland, and while she gave assent to the reporting of the allegations against Fr. Keating, she wasn't otherwise involved. That didn't keep her from bearing the brunt of Fr. Horan's wrath, however. Finally realizing the truth of the situation on his deathbed, Bishop Sheil lifted the excommunication on February 21, 1872.

The next year Sr. Mary went alone to Rome to earn approval of the order's rule and obtain papal support for the Josephites. On meeting her, His Holiness Bl. Pius IX good-naturedly called her the "excommunicated one" and lauded her labors. She then had to wait in Europe until the Josephites received the Vatican's verdict. During this period she wrote in her diary, "Cried myself to sleep. Was so weary of the struggle and felt so utterly alone. Could not pray or say my ordinary rosaries, only offered my weary heart's trials to my God with the wish that he would do his will and make of me what he pleased."[1]

When Rome issued its approval, it called for a mother superior general, which Sr. Mary became after her return to Australia. It also relaxed somewhat the part of the rule that dealt with poverty.

Ironically, papal approval actually brought an increase in episcopal opposition. This was because the Holy See gave administrative power to the superior general, not the bishop. This innovation led to the order's dismissal from several dioceses. For instance, in a meeting around 1876, the bishop of Queensland told Mother Mary that he wanted the sisters but only on his terms. Any who wanted to stay and be under his authority could do so. By 1880 all Josephites had left the territory. In 1883 Adelaide's archbishop Christopher Reynolds launched a commission of investigation. He wanted to bring the Josephites under his thumb or, failing that, destroy them. And so the commission investigated the foundress's alleged alcoholism.

St. Mary did drink alcohol. Regularly. On her doctor's orders. She had dysmenorrhea, which causes debilitating pain during menses. In a day before more effective medications, alcohol seemed the only option. She never abused it. To the archbishop's chagrin, the commission returned a favorable verdict. Nonetheless the archbishop asked Mother Mary to leave his diocese.

So Mother moved to Sydney, where the archbishop staunchly supported the institute. After his death, however, his replacement, Cardinal Patrick Moran, while otherwise supporting the Josephites, was like the other Australian bishops: He couldn't accept in his see a religious institution that was not under his control. Australia's bishops asked Rome to reconsider. The Holy See simply affirmed its previous decision. Even today, this sort of autonomy is totally unique to the Josephites.

Cardinal Moran did succeed in removing Sr. Mary as mother general and replacing her with Sr. Bernard Walsh, who, to assuage the bishops, was appointed by Pope Leo XIII to a ten-year term. Around this time, in 1886, Sr. Mary learned of her mother's drowning in a shipwreck. Did she, Sr. Mary of the Cross, recall what she had written three years earlier? "We have had much sorrow and are still suffering its effects, but sorrow or trial lovingly submitted to do not prevent our being happy—it rather purifies our happiness, and in so doing draws our hearts nearer to God."[2]

Despite or maybe because of her personal trials, Mary gave of herself totally. Once she moved a death row convict to his knees in prayer when he saw the tears streaming in rivulets down her face. Another time, she almost stumbled over a woman languishing in the gutter. Everyone else passing by totally ignored her. After all, since the lady looked like she was nothing more than a low-life lush, she must be, right? It was only after Sr. Mary stopped to talk with her that she discovered that this lady was no drunk. Rather, she had a disease that mimicked intoxication. Learning this, Sr. Mary got that woman help.

After Mother Bernard's death in 1899, Mother Mary once again became superior general, a post she held despite a stroke in 1902 that left her partially paralyzed. The sisters even reelected her in 1905.

When Australian women gained the right to vote in the 1903 elections, Mother Mary wrote her sisters, "Find out who are the members proposed for election and vote for those who are considered most friendly to the Church and to Religion. Every so-called Catholic is not the best man."[3]

Mother Mary died on August 8, 1909. Cardinal Moran, who was with her near the end, said he had assisted at the deathbed of a saint.

WHY ST. MARY DESERVES OUR ATTENTION AND DEVOTION

When God makes clear his will, we are to "be not afraid." In Psalm 23:5 he promises that he makes us safe in our enemies' presence. Whom then should we fear?

This was the level of trust Mother Mary had in God and his promises. So when she found herself unjustly excommunicated, she did not protest a word or refuse to obey. When asked to leave her home archdiocese, she did not protest. She was wholly obedient and loyal to the relevant authorities.

In an age when all manner of authority is easily dismissed, St. Mary Helen MacKillop is a great model for us. She shows us that if God is truly with us, we have nothing ever to fear by obeisance to the authority in our lives (see Acts 5:34–38).

Lord Jesus, help us love you as St. Mary did, so we may do everything you ask. Help us remember that all authority comes from God (see Romans 13:1–7). Give us the humility and strength to follow the example of you and St. Mary by obeying those who have due authority (see Matthew 17:27), even when this seems painful or shameful (see John 19:11).

Bl. Cyprian Michael Iwene Tansi
A Saint Can Come From Anywhere
September 1903–January 20, 1964 • Beatified: March 2, 1998
Memorial: January 20

Quick, think of a saint, any saint. Maybe your favorite saint or the saint after whom your parish is named.

Now, ten to one, if you saw that saint in your mind, he or she probably was white and European. That's perfectly understandable, for the saints most people know come from our Western culture.

However, the word *catholic* means "universal." Jesus said to make disciples of all nations (see Matthew 28:19), and that includes places other than Europe, right? Our current saint came from one of those other places. Furthermore, he is the first African since antiquity to be beatified.

Born September 1903 as Iwene Tansi, he was sent by his animist parents to a school run by the Holy Ghost missionaries. There he accepted the faith, taking the new name Michael at baptism. He worked as a teacher after graduation, but in a short while he discerned a call to the priesthood. He entered the seminary in 1925.

Ordained in 1937, he was one of only ten native priests in all Nigeria. He served the next thirteen years in the diocese of Onitsha, going between the villages on foot or by bicycle. His special focus was working with youth.

One result of this focus is that on All Saints Day 1941, he baptized a nine-year-old local boy who idolized him and wanted to be just like him. Today we call that youngster Cardinal Francis Arinze. For years many thought he would be the first African pope in a millennium.

While Fr. Tansi did great things with his youth, it was at marriage preparation that he particularly excelled. He worked very hard to help those planning their marriages understand the sacredness and uniqueness of the nuptial union. For instance, if a couple wanted him to marry them, he would not let them live together beforehand. Jesus, after all, never intended the sacrament of matrimony to simply be a codification of some preexisting living arrangement. Therefore, requiring men and women to separate until after the wedding enabled Father to stress for them the seriousness and permanency of the conjugal bond. If couples protested that they needed to save money, he found the women shelter elsewhere. Indeed, the value and dignity of women, which has been a constant focus of Christianity, was something Father emphasized.

Fr. Tansi also gave excellent spiritual direction. For instance, he wrote to his houseboy:

> Yourself and your wife should keep always before your eyes that fact that you are creatures, God's own creation. As a man's handiwork belongs to him, so do we all belong to God, and should accordingly have no other will but His. He is a Father, a very kind Father. All his plans are for the good of His children. We may not often see how they are. That does not matter. Leave yourselves in His hands, not for a year, nor for two years, but as long as you have to live on earth. If you confide in Him fully and sincerely He will take special care of you.[1]

One French biography says that Fr. Tansi's ability to excel as a parish priest came not from him but from assiduous prayer, especially prayer before the Blessed Sacrament.

As the 1940s drew to a close, however, Fr. Tansi realized that pastoral work was not his calling, that he was more contemplative than active. So when his bishop called for priests to volunteer to become Trappist monks in England and thereby learn everything involved in establishing a monastery in the diocese, he and another Nigerian priest volunteered. In 1950 they applied for and were accepted into the English monastery of Mount Saint Bernard. On December 8, 1956, Fr. Tansi became fully professed, taking the name Fr. Cyprian, and from then on he lived a life of quiet contemplation.

By 1963 the plans to establish the long-dreamed-of monastery in Nigeria were complete. Fr. Cyprian was to be novice master. If one knows anything about Nigeria, however, it's that ever-simmering political tensions are always a wrong step away from boiling over into full-blown violence. Because of this the monastery's location was changed to Cameroon, which meant that Father would not take part as a founder. Receiving this news left Fr. Cyprian bewildered. He grew very angry, the only time as a monk he was seen to lose his temper. After a short while, though, he reminded himself that this was obviously God's will and that he "should accordingly have no other will but His."[2] To do otherwise would have been spiritually dangerous.

The following January 18, after suffering extreme leg pain, Fr. Cyprian was diagnosed with a blood clot. Found unconscious the next day, he was admitted to a local hospital, having suffered an aortic aneurysm. By the next morning he was dead.

Why Bl. Cyprian deserves our attention and devotion

One of the great things about our religion is that it unifies. It gives everyone the ability to become holy and so attain eternal salvation. There is nothing "African" about Bl. Cyprian's path to sanctity. The things that made him great have been practiced by all great Christians throughout history: fidelity to the teachings of Christ and his Church, prayer, reception of the sacraments, sacrificing oneself for others, and so on. Whether in Africa, Saudi Arabia, Myanmar, Uruguay, or your hometown, growing in holiness by these means is something each of us can do.

Lord Jesus, because of his intense love for you, Bl. Cyprian managed to make ordinary things extraordinary. Through his prayers and example and those of the Blessed Virgin, help us to grow in our zealous love for you. Let this not be a love of feelings but a love of action, sacrifice, and service. May we humbly follow where you lead us. Then give us the grace to trust you, knowing that your plans are only and always for our good.

Bl. Marie-Clémentine Anuarite Nengapeta

The Weaker Sex?

December 29, 1939–December 1, 1964 • Beatified: August 15, 1985

Memorial: December 1

Life often confronts us with bewildering circumstances. We cannot fathom why God would let something happen to us, much less how we will survive the situation. In such circumstances, some reject God and go their own way, not realizing that it is only the power of Christ, who defeated death and ultimately all suffering through his resurrection, that will strengthen them and enable them to endure. And while women are often called the "weaker sex," it is often holy women who disprove this point better than anyone. Take, for example, Bl. Clémentine Nengapeta, a Congolese religious who could say from an early age, "My tears have been my food day and night" (Psalm 42:3).

At the time of Clémentine's birth, the Democratic Republic of the Congo was a Belgian colony, and her animist father had become a soldier in its army, the Force Publique, or FP. When King Leopold II signed Belgium's surrender to the Nazis in 1940, the Belgian government-in-exile operating out of London refused to accept it. It thereby set out to aid the Allied war effort by cobbling together the Free Belgian Forces, which consisted of three naval ships, a number of fighter pilots, a hodgepodge of expatriate subjects, and various units of colonial troops. The largest body of these troops was the FP, which showed great bravery in victorious fighting against Italian forces during the East Africa Campaign, which lasted from 1940 to 1941.

Between 1942 and 1943, the Allies' commanders stationed nine thousand FP troops in Palestine so they could move the British garrison there to fight on other fronts. What Clémentine's father saw during his service in the Holy Land persuaded him to become a Christian. He then wrote his wife and told her to take their daughters to the local

Catholic mission and have them baptized. His wife became a Catholic catechumen, and she and her daughters received baptism in 1943.

Now Anuarite, as she was called at birth, was the fourth of six daughters. When the sixth came along, her father divorced her mother to take another wife, so that he might have a son. (Ironically, his second wife was sterile.) This abandonment by her father was painful for the young girl. Maybe this contributed to her being a sensitive child.

Of just average intelligence, Anuarite had to work extra hard in school and even had to repeat fifth grade, about which some people made painful comments that hurt her deeply. That didn't affect her disposition in the home, however, as she was always very helpful. Part of that came from watching the religious in her village, especially Sr. Ndakala Marie-Anne, her spiritual mother and third-grade teacher. These women instilled in her, from a very early age, a desire to be a religious.

Her mother did not at all support her in this, but this didn't dissuade Anuarite. In fact, at age fourteen she asked the Sisters of the Holy Family for admittance, but they said she was too young. At fifteen, however, she sneaked aboard a truck taking postulants to the local convent. When her mother learned of it, she consented to her daughter's choice of vocation. (See? Even saints can be stubborn and naughty teenagers.) Anuarite, now Sr. Marie-Clémentine, took vows on August 5, 1959. Her parents witnessed the liturgy, and in honor of the occasion they gave two goats to the sisters.

Clémentine made serving and making others happy part of her vocation. In addition to being sacristan and a teacher in the primary school, she took all the jobs others shunned. Indeed, her motto was, "To serve and make them happy," which her grandmother had taught her.

However, when someone purposefully stopped working because they knew Clémentine would pick up the slack, she lashed them with her sharp tongue. Her prickly nature and often uncontrolled anger made her something of a pain. However, she didn't just shrug her shoulders and say, "Oh well, that's how I am." Instead, she worked at dominating her character.

Not long after Sr. Clémentine took her vows, her mother experienced financial difficulties and pressured her to come home and help support her family. To this she replied, "He who puts his hand on the plow and looks back is unworthy of the kingdom of heaven and causes God great sadness."[1] Indeed, she took her consecration to Jesus so seriously that she once physically assaulted a man who was making advances on another sister.

In April 1964 communists and animists revolted against the government, which had achieved independence from Belgium in 1960. Now, the rebels had no use for anyone Christian because half of them didn't believe in God and the other half couldn't understand the Christian conception of God. They also hated the Belgian missionaries because, well, they were Belgian. Congolese priests and religious were also distrusted.

After an initial series of impressive gains, by the end of 1964, the revolutionaries had steadily lost ground and were on the verge of defeat. They became desperate after November 24 when, in a daring rescue operation, Belgian commandoes began freeing captive Belgians and other Westerners. This is the context in which, on November 29, 1964, rebels arrived at the Bafwabaka convent, smashing doors and windows to take all forty-six religious captive. The sisters were told that this was for their own protection from the Americans, who were assisting government forces.

The rebels loaded the sisters on a truck. The sisters knew something was afoot when the truck diverged from the route to where the rebels had told the women they were going. At one point the soldiers stopped the truck and made the women give them all rosaries and crucifixes. They proceeded to smash the holy objects with their boots while shouting blasphemies.

On arriving at their destination, the commander, Col. Ngalo, strode into the room, looked around, and told his subordinate, Col. Pierre Olombe, that he wanted Anuarite for the night. Olombe then separated her from the rest of her sisters, but she said, "I cannot go with your colonel."[2] Col. Olombe told her she had no choice. He would beat her if she refused. Like a mountain glacier, she coolly stood her ground. Enraged, Olombe started insulting her, calling her *motu molayi* (literally, "long head"), a stupid savage.

When he told Ngalo of Clémentine's intransigence, the superior told his subordinate that he must make her do what he wanted or lose his life. Now panic-stricken, Olombe returned to Clémentine and began shouting, beating her, and doing whatever he thought would intimidate her. But his efforts were utterly impotent. Shrugging his shoulders, Ngalo ordered her death.

Olombe then placed Clémentine and a religious he desired, Sr. Bokuma Jean-Baptiste, in a car. Olombe had left the keys in the house and returned inside to get them, leaving the sisters alone in the car. The sisters used this opportunity to attempt an escape. They did not get far, however, and Olombe in his fury proceeded to beat and kick the two women.

Sr. Jean-Baptiste blacked out, but Clémentine remained conscious. As Olombe rained down rapid, hammer-like blows on her, she kept saying, "I forgive you, for you know not what you are doing,"[3] which only increased his fury. Exhausted, he told his soldiers to stab her with bayonets. Then Olombe shot her in the chest.

Her fellow religious took her inside, where she expired a short time later, around 1 AM on December 1. Her last words were *Naivyo nili-vyotaka*, which means something like, "This is what I wanted."[4] The soldiers dumped her body in a common grave. Seven months later it was exhumed, identified by a little statue of Mary in a pocket, and reinterred in the Isiro Cathedral cemetery.

Two years later Olombe was sentenced to death for his crimes. During his captivity his military experience was needed to help repel the rebellion of Belgian farmer Jean Schramme. For his assistance his sentence was commuted to five years.

On his release, wandering, homeless, and hungry, he knocked at the door of Sr. Marie-Clémentine's convent, begging for something to eat. The sisters immediately recognized him. The superior, Mother Léontine, gave him food, for, she said, "Sr. Marie-Clémentine forgave you; we must follow her example."[5]

Bl. Clémentine is the first African woman religious to be beatified. Her parents and three of her sisters were present at her beatification.

WHY BL. CLÉMENTINE DESERVES OUR ATTENTION AND DEVOTION

Bl. Clémentine overcame some pretty tough things in her life. The only reason these trials didn't ruin her is because she clung to the power of the resurrected Christ as a sailor clings to a mast in a storm.

Whether our struggles are similar to or different from hers, each of us struggles. The question is, do we muscle through those on our own, or do we let Jesus' power work for us? The people who chose the first way, we don't much remember them. Bl. Clémentine, however, we will remember forever.

Lord Jesus, through the intercession of Bl. Clémentine, help us remember and better understand St. Paul when he says, "I will all the more gladly boast of my weaknesses, that the power of Christ may rest upon me. For the sake of Christ, then, I am content with weaknesses, insults, hardships, persecutions, and calamities; for when I am weak, then I am strong" (2 Corinthians 12:9–10).

Notes

Sts. Perpetua and Felicity

1. *The Passion of Saints Perpetua and Felicity*, Medieval Sourcebook, Fordham University, http://www.fordham.edu/halsall/source/perpetua.asp.

2. *The Passion of Saints Perpetua and Felicity* 3, Medieval Sourcebook, Fordham University, http://www.fordham.edu/halsall/source/perpetua.asp.

St. Radegund

1. http://pikku-myy.blogspot.com/2010/08/st-radegund-of-poitiers.html.

St. Deicolus of Lure

1. Margaret Stokes, *Three Months in the Forests of France: A Pilgrimage in Search of Vestiges of the Irish Saints in France* (London: George Bell and Sons, 1895), p. 41.

2. Stokes.

3. From www.bartleby.com/210/1/184.html.

St. Fiacre

1. Denise and Jean-Pierre le Dantec, *Reading the French Garden: Story and History* (Boston: MIT Press, 1990), p. 8.

St. Bathilde

1. Antiochan http://www.antiochian.org/node/17361.

St. Willibrord

1. Thomas F.X. Noble and Thomas Head, eds., *Soldiers of Christ: Saints and Saints' Lives from Late Antiquity and the Early Middle Ages*, (University Park, Pa.: Pennsylvania State University Press, 1995), p. 194.

2. From www.fordham.edu/halsall/basis/bede-book5.asp.

St. Gangolf

1. This is also rendered "If Gengulphus can work miracles, then so can my arse." See http://www.gengulphus.org.

2. Translation by author. Original quote: "*S'il pleut le jour de Saint-Gengoul, les porcs auront de glands leur soul*," as found in Baron Otto von Reinsberg-Düringsfeld, *Traditions et légendes de la Belgique* (Brussels: Ferdinand Claasen, Libraire-E'diteur, 1870), vol. 2, p. 327.

3. See Paul VI, *Humanae Vitae* 17.

St. Benoît d'Aniane

1. Isaac Gregory Smith, *A Dictionary of Christian Biography, Literature, Sects, and Doctrines*, William Smith and Henry Wace, eds. (Boston: Little, Brown, 1877), pp. 305–308.

St. Homobonus Tucenghi of Cremona

1. Innocent III, *Quia Pietas*, papal bull (January 13, 1199), as quoted in Régine Pernoud, *Les Saints au Moyen Âge: La sainteté d'hier est-elle pour aujourd'hui?* (Paris: Plon, 1984). Original quote translated in part by the author: "*Deux choses sont requises pour que quelqu'un puisse être réputé saint: la vertu des mœurs et la vérité des signes, c'est-à-dire les œuvres de piété dans la vie et les manifestations des miracles après la mort.*"

St. Bona of Pisa

1. http://www.saintpatrickdc.org/ss/0529.shtml.

Bl. Piero Tecelano

1. See Paul VI, *Populorum et Progressio*; Bl. John Paul II, *Laborem Exorcens*; *Catechism of the Catholic Church,* #1434, 2443–2449.

St. Lydwine of Schiedam

1. Thomas à Kempis, *St. Lydwine of Schiedam, Virgin,* Vincent Scully trans. (London: Burnes and Oates, 1912), p. 15, http://tiny.cc/rda3x.
2. "Pope: Disabled Fully Human, Deserving of Full Rights," Catholic News Agency, March 7, 2006.

Martyrs of Otranto

1. *The Renaissance: God in Man, A.D. 1300 to 1500* (Edmonton, Alta.: Society to Explore and Record Christian History, 2010), p. 131.

Bl. José de Anchieta

1. "The 'Autos' of José de Anchieta," abstract of a paper given by Nola Kortner Aiex at the Annual Kentucky Foreign Language Conference (Lexington, Ky., April 25–27, 1991).

Bl. Sebastián de Aparicio

1. "*Aunque viese más demonios que mosquitos*" (author's translation), http://hispanidad. tripod.com/hechos14.htm.
2. "*A lo que respondió fray Sebastián muy tranquilo: 'Pues si Dios os lo mandó ¿qué aguardáis? Haced lo que Él os manda, que yo estoy muy contento de hacer lo que a Dios le agrada*" (author's translation), http://hispanidad.tripod.com/hechos14.htm.

St. Lorenzo Ruiz

1. http://www.stlorenzoruiz.com/.
2. http://www.all-about-the-virgin-mary.com/lorenzo-ruiz.html.

St. Pedro de San José Betancur

1. Actual quote: "*Dios, no nos trajo a esta tierra…sólo para cuidar al Calvario. Andad y salid de aquí, que hay muchos pobres y necesitados a quienes podéis ser de mucho provecho y en que sirváis a Dios y os aprovechéis de ellos y de uno mismo*" (translation by Stewart Wolfenson and author), http://hispanidad.tripod.com/hechos15.htm.

2. Pope Alexander VII, *Sollicitudo Omnium Ecclesiarum*. In 1854, Bl. Pope Pius IX made the doctrine of the Immaculate Conception a dogma—that is, binding on all believers.

3. Actual quote:*"perdía el juicio...Yo no puedo más / con este misterio.Ya que pierdo el juicio, / Que le Sr. me dé remedio"* (translation by Stewart Wolfenson and author), http://hispanidad.tripod.com/hechos15.htm.

Martyrs of Korea

1. *The New Glories of the Catholic Church*, Fathers of the London Oratory trans. (London: Richardson and Son, 1859), p. 118.

St. Charles Lwanga and Companions

1. John F. Faupel, *African Holocaust:The Story of the Uganda Martyrs* (Nairobi: Paulines Publications Africa, 1962); and "Pope to Honor 22 Negroes," *Milwaukee Sentinel*, July 19, 1969, part 1, p. 24.

2. http://www.op-stjoseph.org/blog/saints_charles_lwanga_and_his_companions_martyrs/.

3. http://www.dacb.org/stories/uganda/lwanga_charles.html.

4. "St. Charles Lwanga and Companions, Martyrs of Uganda," Catholic News Agency, June 3, 2011.

5. http://www.ugandamartyrsshrine.org.ug/martyrs.php?id=1.

6. http://www.safarisgorillas.com/safaris/tours/ugandamartyrstrail.html.

7. Gabriel Gillen, "Saints Charles Lwanga and His Companions, Martyrs," Dominnican Province of St. Joseph, http://tiny.cc/fltic.

8. Kevin Ward, "A History of Christianity in Uganda," http://tiny.cc/qhv4j.

St. Mary Helen MacKillop

1. http://www.marymackillop.org.au/marys-story/challenge.cfm.

2. http://www.marymackillop.org.au/marys-story/challenge.cfm.

3. http://www.marymackillop.org.au/marys-story/influences.cfm.

Bl. Cyprian Michael Iwene Tansi

1. http://faithofthefatherssaintquote.blogspot.com/2006/01/saint-quote-blessed-cyprian-michael.html.

2. http://www.blessedtansi.com/.

Bl. Marie-Clémentine Anuarite Nengapeta

1. www.katolsk.no/biografier/historisk/anengape.

2. *"Je ne peux pal aller chez votre colonel,"* http://www.afriquespoir.com/saints-dafrique/page8.html.

3. http://www.dacb.org/stories/demrepcongo/anuarite_mc.html.

4. http://www.katolsk.no/biografier/historisk/anengape.

5. http://www.dacb.org/stories/demrepcongo/anuarite_mc.html.

ABOUT THE AUTHOR

Brian O'Neel is a frequent guest on the EWTN and Relevant Radio networks. A writer and editor, Brian lives in rural Wisconsin with his wife and six children—all Green Bay Packers fans. He is the author of *39 New Saints You Should Know*.